D0391996

mama knows best

african-american

wives' tales,

myths, and

remedies for

mothers and

mothers-to-be

Chrisena Coleman

Simon & Schuster

SIMON & SCHUSTER
Rockefeller Center
1230 Avenue of the Americas
New York, NY 10020

Copyright © 1997 by Chrisena Coleman
All rights reserved,
including the right of reproduction
in whole or in part in any form.

SIMON & SCHUSTER and colophon are registered trademarks
of Simon & Schuster Inc.

Book design and border illustrations by Bonni Leon-Berman

Illustrations © 1997 by Arinthia Jones

Manufactured in the United States of America

1   3   5   7   9   10   8   6   4   2

Library of Congress Cataloging-in-Publication Data

Coleman, Chrisena.
Mama knows best: African-American wives' tales, myths, and
remedies for mothers and mothers-to-be / Chrisena Coleman.
p.   cm.
1. Afro-American woman—Folklore. 2. Mothers—United
States—Folklore. 3. Traditional medicine—United States—
Formulae, receipts, prescription. 4. Tales—United States.
I. Title.
GR111.A47C65   1997
398'.082—dc21   97-746
                                                          CIP

ISBN 0-684-83426-X

This publication contains the opinions and ideas of its author and of various contributors. It is intended to provide interesting information on the subject matter covered. It is sold with the understanding that the author and publisher are not engaged in rendering medical or other professional services in the book. If the reader requires personal medical or health assistance or advice, a competent professional should be consulted.

The author and publisher specifically disclaim any responsibility for any liability, loss, or risk, personal or otherwise, which is incurred as a consequence, directly or indirectly, of the use and application of any of the contents of this book.

THIS BOOK IS DEDICATED TO:

My precious son, Jordan Christopher Coleman. Without you, this book would have been written by someone else. You have no idea how much your birth has inspired me. May the spirit and love of God guide you always.

My parents, Dorothy and Wilbert Coleman. Thank you for always understanding my desire and thirst to write—even when I was a child and wrote on your walls, lampshades, and spray painted my name on the wall outside our apartment complex. Your unconditional love, encouragement, and strong sense of family are blessings. You are my role models—my heroine and my hero. Thanks for believing in me and helping make all my dreams come true.

My brother, Maurice Coleman, aka Mustafa. Thanks for your prayers and for cheering me on, even when you couldn't cheer for yourself. *I love ya, man!*

My grandpa, John Miller. Thanks for investing in my future. Your commitment to the family is a treasure.

acknowledgments

To the rest of the family: Aunt Glo, Odessa, Aunt Julie, Aunt Hortense and Uncle Gene, Mama Pearson, Cheryl, Erika, Aunt Mae, Cousin Mildred, Aunt Elzeal, Mama Hattie, Aunt Frances, Aunt Barbara, Loretta, Karen and Aunt Doris, Ruby, Edwena, Wilemena, Aunt Esther Clay, the Reverend Gregory Jackson, and the Mt. Olive Church family.

Here's to good friends: New and old, near and far, thanks for baby-sitting, proofreading, praying for me, and understanding my burning desire to write. Your patience, support, and love is invaluable. To: Linda, Veronica, Denene, Amy, Shelley, Angelita, Joyce, Charise, Adriane, Sam, Natalie, Tonya, Kim, Adrienne, Lesvia, Pam, Holly, Stacy, Robyn, Kathy, Gwynne, Cindy, Lanecia, Andrea, Rhea, Dayna, Faigi, Karen Lombardi, Madeline Carrino, Miss Joan, and Mrs. Joyce Watson.

To my little Mama's helpers: Shonna and Jade—thank you!

Thanks to everyone who helped make this book possible: librarians, nursing home residents, friends, friends and relatives of friends, and women across the country.

My agent: Eileen Cope, of Lowenstein-Morel & Associates. And I thought this would make a good magazine piece, remember? Thanks for your vision and friendship.

Last but not least, my editor, Annie Hughes O'Connor: Working with you was wonderful. Let's do it again, and again, and again . . . and then some!

In God We Trust

contents

Introduction 11

contents

PART THREE
motherhood
95

introduction

Here's to Mamas-to-be, Mamas, and grandMamas every-where. As a first-time Mama-to-be, I waited with bated breath to attend my monthly doctor appointments and I followed the instructions of my obstetrician, Dr. Wendy Hurst, to a tee. I struggled to swallow those big yellow prenatal vitamins, gulped down eight glasses of water a day, cut down my salt intake, and ate as many fruits and vegetables as I possibly could. I walked more than I had in my entire life and popped a Tylenol every time I had an ache, pain, or sniffle. Just like Dr. Hurst told me to.

Yet, as my nine-month journey to motherhood progressed, I found myself depending less on clinical advice and more on my female relatives and friends. Now that I am the proud Mama of a baby boy, Jordan, it's those very same people that I rely on most for tips and advice on mothering.

Throughout my pregnancy, my own Mama, female friends, and relatives listened closely as I complained about mood swings, body changes, aches, pains, and other prenatal worries.

"What did your doctor say?" they'd always ask, and they'd listen as I explained what Dr. Hurst suggested and prescribed for each ache and ailment. After assuring me they respected Dr. Hurst's medical expertise, they also reminded me that what I really needed was some good, old-fashioned advice from Mamas like themselves.

And so, each woman shared with me the old wives' tales, myths, stories, anecdotes, and down-home remedies that they had been told. Stories that had been passed down from great-grandMama to grandMama to Mama.

Though skeptical at first, I welcomed each and every one, tried dozens, ignored some, and jotted them all down in my notebook. Some tales are very old and others are new, but the important thing is they might work for you.

Many of the old wives' tales and cures originated during the days of slavery, when pregnant slaves did not have access to medical attention. They had no choice but to put their faith in God and look to the heavens for help. And, of course, to rely on their own Mama, knowing that she was indeed a walking, talking, breathing wealth of knowledge— because she had already been through it.

Mama especially remembered the traditions of pregnancy that were transported from African tribes. As slaves were snatched from the Motherland and brought to the New World against their will, they carried with them long-standing traditions and beliefs about pregnancy and motherhood.

Throughout slavery, Mamas passed on their suggestions and recollections to expectant mothers on different plantations. And, ultimately—between dances, sing-alongs, church services, or any place the females could find to talk freely— these old wives' tales and cure-all remedies were passed on by word of mouth.

Because slaves were forbidden to learn to read or write, few of these tales were written down, but instead were told over and over again throughout the generations. With each telling, the exact wording would inevitably change a bit. But although the stories have been tailored, distorted, amended, even updated over the years, they remain a vital and important tradition for today's black Mamas and Mamas-to-be.

Take it from me. I like to think of myself as a modern

woman—a single, professional mother—but I definitely came to depend on stories from my own Mama, family members, and friends. In fact, every time I turned around, someone was telling me what to do. When I complained that my breasts were tender, sore, and swollen, my cousin Erika told me to put a chilled collard green or cabbage leaves in my bra to relieve the pain.

"It's some old country tale," Erika explained. "But it worked for me. I kept a head of cabbage in my refrigerator during my pregnancy."

Even when I did not want advice, people were constantly telling me what to do and what *not* to do. Dr. Hurst told me to limit coffee drinking to one cup a day, if at all. The caffeine, she warned, could increase my chances of miscarriage or possibly cause harmful side effects. My aunts told me to steer away from it, too—but they believed it for another reason: the coffee would make my baby a darker shade of black.

I was forbidden to cry or yell because they said my baby would be cranky and cry all the time. So I forced myself to maintain a cheerful disposition—even when my hormones were going nuts.

After Jordan made his grand entrance into this world, the madness continued.

Jordan's pediatrician told me not to worry about my son's herniated belly button. He said it would go in once Jordan's stomach muscles were developed. But Mama swore that only a bellyband or a silver dollar would do the trick. After all, that's what her Mama told her—and her Mama was always right.

And the spoonful of cod-liver oil Jordan takes every morning? That's to keep colds and germs away. At least that's what Dolly Terrell, the nanny who helped me take care of Jordan during my first weeks of Mamahood, told me.

Each time I heard a new tale, I shared it with my own Mama. We laughed at a lot of them, but my Mama confessed that she believed in many of them, too.

"I know you pay your doctors for advice and you want to listen to them, but Mama knows best," she said repeatedly. "If it worked for your grandmother and your great-grandmother, it should be good enough for you."

As usual, Mama was right. I was so intrigued by all the tales that I began collecting them. I also prodded the memories of my friends and family and interviewed dozens of black women to find out what they were told when they were in the family way.

The more women I spoke to and the more research I collected, the more I learned about pregnancy, motherhood, and, most of all, the richness of the Afrocentric culture. Black women were our strength of the past and continue to hold our hope for the future.

Many of these tales are offbeat, some are downright funny, and some really worked for me. My hope is that Mamas-to-be and Mamas of all ages will sit back and enjoy—and perhaps reach into their own memories of pregnancy and motherhood.

Mama Knows Best is our motherly link with women of color, who started many of these tales and passed them on to family members, friends, and now to you. These pregnancy and maternal traditions have thrived for hundreds of years, thanks to great-grandMa, grandMa, and, of course, Mama, who truly does know best!

PART ONE

pregnancy

Welcome to the wonderful world of Mamahood—an honor so special that it takes a full nine months to receive your membership. Having a baby is a gift from God, so enjoy it. But keep in mind, now that you're pregnant, almost everything you do—I'm talking eating, sleeping, walking, and breathing—could have an effect on your baby. But don't worry, I'm here to help smooth the way. So sit back and relax.

chapter one

so, you're gonna
be a mama

When I was a teenager growing up in Hackensack, New Jersey, in the 1970s, most young girls were still pure and innocent. Sure, there were a few hotties who became teenage Mamas, but, for the most part, it was highly unusual.

With that in mind, my Mama never had the famous talk with me about the birds and the bees. In fact, the only thing I remember her telling me about sex was: "If you play with fire, you get burnt!"

I took my Mama's advice literally and I was afraid to light matches for a long time. To tell you the truth, it took me years to finally figure out the real message she was trying to convey to me.

And, of course, I am not alone. Mamas have been telling their daughters all sorts of old wives' tales and myths about sex for generations in an attempt to keep their girls safe. You know the ones: If you slow-dance with a boy . . . kiss him . . . have sex before you're married . . . or stay out after midnight, you'll get pregnant. Sound familiar?

These messages were clearly misleading, but they seemed to serve a purpose at the time. Well, some girls may have believed those tales in the old days, but today's girls are much smarter. However, after talking with black women across the country, I heard a lot of unique tales, superstitions, and myths about how to get pregnant—many of which were news to me. . . .

Mama's Surefire Ways to Get Pregnant

◆ If you lay your man's hat on the bed, you will get pregnant.

◆ If you let a pregnant woman comb your hair, you will become pregnant.

◆ If you sit in a chair after a pregnant woman, you will get pregnant.

◆ If you have sex when there's a full moon, you will get pregnant.

◆ If three women sleep together in the same bed, one of them will become pregnant shortly after.

◆ If you have sex in the middle of a thunderstorm, you will become pregnant.

◆ If three women braid a child's hair, the youngest woman will become pregnant.

◆ If you swallow too many watermelon seeds, you will become pregnant.

If You Dream About Fish, Someone Close to You Is Expecting

or years, my girlfriend Veronica has been telling me that every time she dreams about fish, it turns out someone she knows is pregnant.

Veronica's grandmother, Louise Barnes, passed this old wives' tale down to her claiming it originated in the South. She, too, had a history of predicting pregnancies whenever she dreamt about fish. The dreams always vary: whether they dream about fish swimming upstream, a goldfish in a bowl, or even a group of friends eating porgies at a fish fry, no matter! They swear, as long as the fish appears, someone is expecting.

I thought Veronica was losing it, at first, but she backed up her dreaming with a solid track record. The night before our friend Rosie announced she was with child, Veronica had a fish dream. Another time she dreamt about fish and her friend Gladys called from Atlanta to say she was in the family way, hoping this one, the fourth, was the little girl she had always wanted.

This old wives' tale is not just a family thing for Veronica and her granny—Mamas that I interviewed from Tallahassee to Phoenix, with family in the South, also believe this tale.

Still not convinced? Okay, I don't blame you, but listen up. One night, Veronica announced that she had another one of those fish dreams and we spent hours trying to figure out who could possibly have a bun in the oven.

We went down a list of likely college mates who were married and a few who lived on the wild side. Then we thought about people in our families. Nah! We could not come up with anyone.

"I *know* that someone is pregnant," Veronica kept telling me. "It's just a matter of time before I figure out who it is."

Veronica's insistence started to get me nervous. After all, I confided to Veronica, my breasts were a little sore and my period *was* a few days late.

"Aaaa-haa!" Veronica said as if she was Sherlock Holmes. "It's you. You must have a little bun in the oven."

I thought she was being ridiculous, but Veronica was so adamant about it that she convinced me to take a pregnancy test. It was the plus sign! I was pregnant!

Who'da thunk it? Neither one of us. So I took the pregnancy test over and over again, just to be sure. By the sixth test, I was finally convinced. Now I am a believer. Every time Veronica dreams about fish, I just sit back and wait for someone to make the announcement.

The Pregnancy Pulse

ne day, my cousin Diane was walking down a crowded Manhattan street when she ran into an old family friend, Ella. The women hadn't seen each other for at least five years, and hugged with surprise and delight.

They walked a few blocks, catching up on each other's families and lives, but Diane noticed that Ella kept staring at her neck. It became so obvious that Diane finally came out and asked: "Why do you keep staring at my neck? Is there a bug or something on me?"

Ella just smiled.

"Oh, there's a bug all right," she said. "It's obvious that you've been bitten by the love bug. Congratulations! You must be so excited."

Diane didn't have a clue as to what the woman was talking about. "What love bug?" Diane asked.

"The pregnancy love bug, of course," Ella answered.

"But I am *not* pregnant," Diane replied.

"Are you sure about that?" Ella said, grinning from ear to ear. "I can see the double pulse in your neck—that means you are having a baby. Hasn't your Mama ever told you about the double pulse?"

Diane smiled politely and insisted that it was just an old wives' tale.

"Hate to disappoint you, but I'm really not pregnant," Diane said.

The women exchanged telephone numbers and parted. But as Diane made her way home, she couldn't help wonder if there was any truth to it. By now, a little curious, she stopped at a pharmacy and purchased a pregnancy test, if nothing else, just to prove Ella wrong, and she hurried home to take it.

Sure enough, the test was positive. Still not convinced, Diane went to the doctor for a blood test, and he, too, confirmed that she was pregnant. Ella was right, and Diane couldn't have been happier.

Diane picked up the phone to call her Mama, but decided to call Ella first with the good news.

"Hi, darling, I knew you would be calling," Ella said. "My Mama told me that you can always tell if a black woman is pregnant by the double pulse in her neck. Congratulations again, Diane. I know you will be a wonderful Mama."

When Someone in the Family Dies, They Are Making Room for a New Arrival

axine, an eighty-five-year-old woman from Georgia, affectionately called GrandMa Maxie by her grandkids, lived a long and happy life, but just before she passed away, she called for her great-granddaughter, Darlene, to come to her bedside. Darlene was pregnant and GrandMa Maxie wanted to rub her belly to bring the baby good luck.

"GrandMa loves you, Darlene. I'd like to stay 'round to meet your baby, but I am tired. Take good care of this precious gift from God. And when you tell him all about GrandMa Maxie, be sure to tell him I had to leave the world in order to make room for his arrival."

Darlene cried, but GrandMa Maxie told her not to fret.

"The fact that I lived long enough to see four grandchildren, three great-grandchildren, and one great-great-grandchild is a blessing in itself. Be happy you had me as long as you did and wipe those tears."

Two days later, Darlene gave birth to a boy named Matthew. As soon as Darlene was released from the hospital, she took him to see GrandMa Maxie.

GrandMa Maxie smiled at Matthew and rubbed his tiny little hands.

"Make your Mama proud of you, and GrandMa Maxie will see you again one day in heaven."

Shortly after GrandMa Maxie went to heaven. And every now and then, Darlene reminds Matthew that GrandMa Maxie moved into heaven so she could make room in the world for him.

chapter two

cravings

Cravings are some of the first symptoms a pregnant woman experiences and they are not just in a Mama-to-be's imagination. They are indeed real and must be satisfied. Whether it's shrimp cocktail at the break of day or maple syrup–soaked pancakes at midnight, a pregnant woman should never be denied food. At least that's what I heard a friend say in the early weeks of my pregnancy and I never forgot it.

Each time I wanted to chow down, I used those words, "*a pregnant woman should never be denied food*," to coax friends and colleagues to pig out with me. Many women I interviewed said they "had a taste" for strange combinations, foods they'd only eaten as a child, and, in some cases, foods they had never even tried before they were pregnant.

It sounds kind of unusual, but it's the *honest-to-God truth*—cravings are just an inexplicable condition that confuse a Mama-to-be's taste buds for the first four months of pregnancy.

So don't worry when you all of a sudden want to eat kooky combinations of hot and spicy, sweet and sour, or international cuisine—it comes with the territory.

Pickles and Ice Cream

 t's four o'clock in the morning. Wake up your man and tell him to grab his coat and hat. It's time to make a run—a jar of Vlasic crispy sour dills and a triple scoop of Vanilla Swiss Almond Häagen Dazs.

Sound familiar? That's the modern-day version of the pickles-and-ice-cream cliché. But hold on, ladies, if you thought pickles and ice cream was bad, check out this list of cravings I compiled after asking dozens of Mamas what they craved.

Top-Fifteen Most Unusual Cravings

1. A turkey and provolone Blimpie and pork fried rice.
2. Spicy buffalo chicken wings and a caramel sundae.
3. Sardines and grape jelly on crackers.
4. Neck bones with spaghetti and grits.
5. Collard greens, fried shrimp, and scrambled eggs.
6. Smothered pork chops and French toast.
7. Tuna fish with cheese and waffles.
8. Bananas, stewed tomatoes, and fried okra.
9. French fries with cheese sauce and maple syrup.
10. Microwave popcorn topped with chocolate syrup.
11. Pineapple chunks and marshmallows with gravy.
12. Chocolate ice cream and watermelon.
13. Potato chips and whipped cream.
14. Toast with mustard and orange marmalade.
15. Creamed corn and corned beef hash.

African-American Pregnant Women May Crave Starch

Pregnant women do eat a lot of unusual combinations, but this one takes the cake. When I was a little girl, I watched a pregnant friend of the family eat something white and crunchy out of a small blue and white cardboard box, a little bigger than a Cracker Jack box. The way she was munching down, I figured it was sugar cubes or something sweet and delicious.

The minute she put the box down, I admit it, I snuck and ate a cluster. Boy, was I surprised. It was nasty! Tasted like chalk. I knew there was no way that was candy and assumed it must have been a special medicine for pregnant women.

I told Mama and she laughed. "It is Argo starch," Mama chuckled. Yuk, I gagged. Why would anyone eat starch? And why did Mama think it was so funny?

When today's pregnant women crave starch, most of them try to fulfill it by eating rice and potatoes. In the past, though, pregnant women craved the real thing—the same starch used to iron clothes.

Luckily, Cousin Mildred, the matriarch of our family, filled me in: "It has something to do with a deficiency of iron and vitamin B, and African-American women have been craving it for generations."

So, if starch is what you happen to crave, don't worry. Personally, I'd try stocking up on rice and potatoes first— and if that doesn't cut it, go for the Argo. If it worked for our ancestors, it just might work for you.

A Taste of Africa at Home

Down in the South, where the earth is great;
it's surprising to hear what some pregnant women ate.
Sara Jean ate it from a bowl and Mesha ate from her hand;
these Mamas-to-be enjoyed eating the land.

"No pickles and ice cream for us," that's what they'd say;
"We'd rather snack on dirt and clumps of red clay."

It's gritty, it's chalky, and ooh-so-sweet;
a favorite that West African women used to eat.

raving red clay and dirt may sound hard to believe, but it is a tradition that began among pregnant women in West Africa long before the days of slavery. Nobody knows exactly how or why these cravings started, but when West Africans were brought to this country as slaves, the tradition continued. These nonfood cravings are known as "geophagy" or "pica."

It was not uncommon for pregnant slaves to be seen munching on dirt while working in the fields. Some slave owners feared it would make their slaves sick, and often put muzzles over their mouths to stop them. Yet, even after slavery was abolished, black women in rural areas of the South continued to crave clay and dirt, and shared the unique tradition with other women.

I'm told there are still places in the South, such as Mississippi, where cars continue to line up at popular sites and people dig dirt and clay that is later consumed by pregnant women. Some say the sweetest clay comes from around trees, while others say the richest dirt is found on hilltops.

Women who eat clay and dirt make it clear that not just any earth will do. There are prime locations around the country where dirt and clay are choice—and they don't just spoon it from the ground and into their mouths. A small amount usually fulfills the craving.

Though eating the earth might seem out of the ordinary by today's standards, I still managed to round up a slew of African-American women who hailed from the southern states and still craved a taste from our Motherland when they were pregnant. Here are some recipes that women shared with me:

Mama used to crush clusters of red and white clay that she scooped up from a deserted road near her house. She'd bring it over to my house and I'd sprinkle it over a big dish of chocolate ice cream.

Fanny-Mae, Durham, North Carolina

The only way to eat dirt is to bake it in the oven for a few hours and add a little salt and vinegar.

Sandy, Montgomery, Alabama

I like my clay mixed with hot sauce and ketchup.

Annie, Wachula, Florida

When I had my first child, I always topped my rice and gravy with dirt. The second time around, I dipped lumps of clay in chocolate syrup and ate it.

Edna Lee, Pine Bluff, Arkansas

After moving from Mississippi to Chicago, I'd get Mama to mail me a box of red clay when I was pregnant. You see it was not fashionable to eat clay, so I'd have to sneak it.

Bessie, Morgantown, West Virginia

Mama and her sisters ate dirt and clay when they were pregnant because it was a tradition passed down by mothers who worked in the fields. So when I was pregnant with my son, Mama made up a bowl of trail mix—raisins, nuts, and small lumps of clay.

Selma, Elyria, Ohio

Aunt Marley Mae started me eating creamy white clay when I was pregnant. We would mix the clay with hot water, nutmeg, sugar, and a little vanilla.

Greta, Asheville, North Carolina

As the story has been told in our family, generation after generation, my great-grandmother ran out of clay one day when she was pregnant. She was too tired to venture down by the river to replenish her stock. So she began nibbling away at her chimney, which was made of clay and straw. By the end of her pregnancy, great-grandmother had eaten so much of the chimney's clay that it caved in.

Shirley, Newark, New Jersey

Don't Be Surprised If You Suddenly Crave Food from Your Childhood

heila, a first-time mom from Manhattan, hadn't eaten a peanut-butter-and-jelly sandwich since she was a child. But during her first trimester, she couldn't get enough of them and ate them morning, noon, and night. Sheila's grandmother assured her it was perfectly normal. "Many pregnant women crave food from their childhood," she explained. "Cravings vary depending on what foods women associate with their childhood."

To make Sheila feel better, she gave her a few examples. Her friend Carol craved rice with milk, sugar, and butter because that's what she ate growing up in Asheville, North Carolina, in the 1920s.

Blanche, a native of Brooklyn, craved a bowl of tomato soup and an apple-butter sandwich, just like the ones her Mama used to make in the 1940s.

A woman named Ernesta longed for food from her native Jamaica, and not curry chicken and beef jerk, but the taste of a cereal called Ceralac. She searched the grocery stores in Los Angeles, but could never find it. Finally, Ernesta was craving it so badly she called her Mama in Montego Bay and had her ship a few boxes.

So, ladies, if you happen to crave something that brings you back to childhood, don't fret. Whether it's animal crackers, ravioli, or good ol' peanut butter and jelly, you are not alone. It's just the kid in you—literally—that's shining through.

Mamas-to-Be May Develop Aversions to Their Favorite Foods

 f the taste, smell, or sight of your favorite food or drink suddenly turns your stomach, don't be alarmed—it's probably only temporary, just another lovely symptom that comes with pregnancy.

You see, in the first months of pregnancy, some women have aversions to foods they love most. Though steak is one of my all-time favorites, it turned my stomach during my pregnancy. I can't tell you why, but the sight and smell of it made me sick to my stomach.

Alcohol, too, especially tequila, made me nauseous. During my first weeks of pregnancy, I was assigned to cover the O. J. Simpson murder trial in Los Angeles for the *New York Daily News*. At the time, I was only six weeks pregnant and I hadn't yet told my bosses that I was expecting. Thanks to my weak stomach, however, I had people's eyebrows raised in suspicion almost immediately.

At the end of each day, a bunch of journalists would get together for dinner. My coworker Amy was the only one who knew I had a bun in the oven, so she understood why I ordered cranberry and orange juice while everyone else ordered cocktails. Though I did my best to hang with the pack, one journalist ordered a strawberry margarita with a double shot of Cuervo Gold tequila with dinner *every night*.

Although I loved tequila and had drunk my share of it in the past, during my pregnancy, the smell of it made me sick—literally. Each night, when the margarita arrived at the table, I had to run into the ladies' room to be sick. For some reason, tequila had taken on the smell of gasoline. Yuk!! After three nights of this, Amy finally told Ms. Strawberry Margarita that the smell of her tequila made me sick. She didn't take too kindly to it. Each night, when we called her for dinner, she told us that she had made other plans.

Amy wanted to let the tequila-drinking reporter in on my pregnancy so she wouldn't think I was a total witch. I said no because I hadn't even told my editor—knowing that reporters have a reputation of having big mouths, I did not want to share my secret with her.

When I returned to New York, I called the reporter and explained that I was pregnant and had developed an aversion to tequila. We were able to laugh about it, but she did admit that she thought I was a bit strange.

After I gave birth, the reporter sent me a beautiful gift basket with baby booties, bottles, rattles, and a bottle of tequila. I still have the tequila and the card that reads: "I hope the sight of it doesn't make you sick." Everyone wants to know when I'm going to open the bottle, but I couldn't tell you. I never did get my taste back for tequila. I think I am going to wait for her to get pregnant; maybe she will have the same aversion that I did.

A Donut a Day May Keep Cravings Away, But the Calories Will Stay

y poor friend Carol had the misfortune to crave chocolate frosted donuts from a local donut shop. She just had to have one every day during her pregnancy. The donut became part of her daily ritual. She practiced law from her home office, but before she met with clients, Carol would drive fifteen minutes for her daily fix.

Most days, Carol ate only one donut, but there were days when she had more—a lot more. The way we calculated it, Carol ate five hundred chocolate frosted donuts during her pregnancy. That's more than 200,000 calories—empty calories—that her metabolism couldn't break down quickly enough.

Carol gained fifty pounds during her pregnancy, and although she didn't believe all the extra weight came from the donuts, there was no doubt they were a major contributor. Along with the cravings for the donuts, Carol also developed an aversion to the healthy foods she consumed regularly before she was pregnant.

Her son will be celebrating his third birthday this year, but it's unlikely that Carol will want to eat any cake—she's still trying to lose the last twelve pregnancy pounds and swears she will never eat another donut in her life.

If You Overeat During Pregnancy, Your Baby Will Have an Enormous Appetite

kay, it's embarrassing, but I can vouch for this one. During my pregnancy, I ate everything in sight.

Aunt Julie is a caterer and every weekend I had a reserved spot on her couch to sample racks of soul food—fried chicken, collard greens, barbecue spareribs, corn bread, peach cobbler, and anything that went out the door.

Yummy, yummy, it was good for my tummy. I became her official taster and I am not lying when I tell you I loved it all. Aunt Julie warned me that my insatiable appetite would mark my baby and he, too, would eat all the time.

"Oh, that's just an old wives' tale," I'd say, laughing.

But I am not laughing anymore. From the moment Jordan came into this world, he gobbled up everything in sight. He can gulp down a ten-ounce bottle in less than five minutes, and a five-ounce bottle in two and a half minutes, without coming up for air.

At seven months old, he woke up from a deep sleep because he got a whiff of my microwave popcorn. Not only did he sit up, Jordan crawled over to me with his mouth wide open. I could hardly believe it—my son was an eating machine. What will I do when he's a teenager?

Aunt Julie said I cursed him with my pregnancy appetite and she was right. So listen up, unless you are prepared to have a baby who is capable of eating you out of house and home, heed Aunt Julie's advice and try to control your appetite.

Cravings Reveal a Lot About Your Baby

◆ If you crave collard greens, your baby will have a lot of soul.

◆ If you crave fresh fish, your baby will be smart.

◆ If you crave garlic, your baby will have a strong personality.

◆ If you crave ice, your baby will be cold-natured and will always need an extra layer of clothing.

◆ If you crave liver, your baby will be strong.

◆ If you crave chocolate, your baby will have a pleasant and sweet personality.

◆ If you crave onions, your baby will cry a lot.

◆ If you crave chitterlings, your baby will have a lot of guts and courage.

◆ If you eat strawberries or spaghetti sauce, your baby will be born with a bright red birthmark on his body. (Okay, this one is the gospel! I ate both and Jordan has a big red splash on the nape of his neck.)

You Are What You Eat—the Same Goes for Baby

- If you eat a lot of hot sauce, your baby will be mean, evil, and hateful.

- If you drink a lot of milk, your baby's bones and teeth will be healthy.

- If you eat pepper, you will burn your unborn baby's eyes.

- If you swallow fruit seeds, your baby will always like that particular fruit.

- If you drink a lot of water, your baby will enjoy taking baths and showers.

- If you pig out on pickles, your baby will have a sour disposition.

- If you eat pasta all the time, your baby will be very energetic.

- If you eat a lot of carrots, your baby will have great vision.

chapter three

dreams, nightmares, & prayers

My friends warned me that I'd start having dreams about my baby around my seventh month of pregnancy. They were right! While many of my dreams were pleasant, I admit that I did have a few downright crazy ones.

The more I talked about my dreams, the more dreams other women shared with me, and now I want to pass some along to you.

Pregnancy Dreams Can Come True If the Ability to Believe Is Within You

Denise wanted a baby girl so badly that she started having dreams about her daughter. In her dreams, her little angel had golden-brown skin, curly black hair, almond-shaped eyes, and a pudgy little nose. A month later, Denise gave birth to a little boy, and he looked nothing like the baby in her dream. No almond-shaped eyes, no pudgy little nose. No little girl.

Instead, she had a beautiful son with fair skin and sandy hair, and he was by far the cutest little guy she'd ever seen. Denise was, without a doubt, in love with her little man. But the dream about her baby girl seemed so real that it stayed with her for years.

She could still picture her funny-face daughter, smiling, cooing, and crying—and that same baby came back to her in recurring dreams year after year.

Three years later, Denise gave birth to her second child. This time, it was the baby girl with golden-brown skin, curly black hair, almond eyes, and a pudgy nose—the same baby who stole her heart in her dream.

You may not believe me. But take it from a Mama who knows. Her baby girl stepped out of her dreams and into her life, and she has no one to thank but her faith and belief that some dreams really *do* come true.

The Anticipation of Baby Brings Bizarre Dreams

 know I just told you that if you want something badly enough, sometimes dreams can
come true. Well, I am also here to set the
record straight. Not everyone has cute little dreams like
Denise. In fact, it is common for pregnant women to suffer
from nightmares—it is an unconscious way of expressing
your fears.

One night, I had the most bizarre dream—I went into
labor and a caravan of family members and friends drove
me to the hospital around the corner from my house. We
jumped out of the cars and paraded into the labor and delivery room.

Within minutes, I had given birth. No cold sweats, no
pain, and no epidural. I wanted to see my bundle of joy.
Where's my baby? Did I have a girl or a boy? Mama looked
at me and smiled.

"You had a waffle," Mama boasted.

"A waffle?"

Aunt Glo popped out from the back of the crowd with a
mile-long grin: "Your cousin Cheryl was a waffle when she
was born."

"A waffle?"

I was in shock, but Aunt Glo reassured me that it was
perfectly normal to give birth to a waffle. She said it would
turn into a baby if I watered it.

When I woke up, I was so relieved. I told my mother
about the dream, and she just laughed and asked if I had
been craving waffles.

A few nights later, I had another totally weird dream: I

gave birth to a grasshopper smack dab in the middle of the newsroom at the *Daily News,* where I work. As soon as I delivered and held the green insect for a few minutes, my editor, Jerry Schmetterer, sent me out to cover a breaking news story. When I returned, my baby grasshopper was gone. Reporter Chris Oliver, who sat next to me, had put the grasshopper in my top desk drawer because it was crying too loudly and he was trying to write a story on deadline.

I opened the drawer and the grasshopper was gasping for air. I started screaming at the top of my lungs—my grasshopper seemed to be dying. Another editor and photo assistant ran over to give it mouth-to-mouth.

It took some doing, but they revived my baby grasshopper. Once I knew my grasshopper was okay, I plucked Chris on the back of his head, vowing he would never baby-sit my grasshopper again.

Once again, I awoke in a cold sweat. Everyone I told agreed this dream was the result of stress. Pregnancy and holding down a job is no easy task, especially when you are a New York City reporter. But, thankfully, pregnancy is not as scary or bizarre as the dreams I had. So rest assured, if you are having nightmares about your baby, you are not alone. Just try to think peaceful thoughts before you go to bed each night and pray sweet dreams come to you.

When You Dream About Death, It Signifies a New Life

 ix days before Jordan was due, I woke up in a panic. I had a nightmare that Jordan's father died, unexpectedly. As soon as I woke up, I called his father, and thankfully he was fine. The dream seemed so vivid, however, that I was still shook up and called my friend Veronica.

No sooner had I told her about my dream than Veronica blurted out: "When you dream about death, it usually means life. You are probably going to have the baby today."

Yeah, right!! I was a week early, and from what everyone had been telling me, the first baby is *always late*. I wasn't buying into Veronica's dream theory this time. I had heard enough. But, once again, Veronica proved me wrong.

Literally, two minutes later, I felt a sharp, stinging pain in my stomach. Veronica was sure my baby was on the way and insisted I rush to the hospital, but I refused. The pain subsided so we just kept on yip-yapping about what my dream could have possibly meant.

Next thing I knew, my water broke, and, sure enough, I was going into labor. Hey, Veronica, I hear the psychic hotline folks are looking for workers. I'm going to sign you up, girl!

African-American Mama-to-Be Prayer

Now I lay me down to rest,
may baby lay comfy in my nest.

A healthy boy or healthy girl,
another blessing into this world.

If dreams really do come true,
Mama dreams only the best for you.

Ten fingers, ten toes, and a heart of gold,
intelligent and kind with a God-fearing soul.

I had a dream that you were already here,
Mama smothered you with kisses,
tender love, and lots of care.

We played by day and read books at night,
You looked just like GrandMa—such a pretty sight.

You learned about the family and our African kin,
You laughed, and smiled, and gave me a big grin.

The happiest baby in all the land,
A perfect shade of brown, just like a honey tan.

Now it's time to really sleep,
I pray all dreams are ours to keep.

is it a girl . . .
or is it a boy?

Maybe it's a girl; maybe it's a boy;
whatever the sex, it's sure to bring joy.

Everyone has their own way to tell;
but sometimes these theories don't work so well.

Here's a list of theories and clues;
that some African-American mothers may want to use.

The Baby Guessing Game

rying to guess the sex of the baby has become a favorite pastime of some expectant Mamas and their friends. There are all kinds of old wives' tales, myths, and tests that may help you find out the sex of your unborn child. While the ultrasound is one of the best indicators, even its accuracy is not 100 percent; and some Mamas opt not to find out.

So if you are curious about the sex of your baby but don't want to be told by your doctor, try these African-American tests and traditions. What the heck, even if you do opt for the ultrasound, try these out to see how accurate they really are:

- If a Mama-to-be picks up a baby girl and she starts crying, the Mama will have a son. If she holds a baby boy and he starts crying, she will have a daughter.

- Thread a needle and hold it over a pregnant woman's stomach. If the needle moves side to side, the Mama is carrying a boy. If it moves up and down, it's a baby girl inside.

- Flip a coin. If it lands on heads, chances are you will have a girl. If it lands on tails, expect a boy.

- Break a wishbone. If you walk away with the largest part, you are carrying a boy. If you have the small portion, you will have a girl.

Even if you really don't care whether it's a girl or boy—as long as he or she is healthy—women will insist they can tell you what you're having just by looking at you. Here are the most common clues. . . .

You Must Be Having a Boy Because...

You haven't lost your looks, boys preserve your beauty.
You're carrying high and your stomach is very round.
Women have become very friendly and warm toward you.
You are hungrier than you've ever been in your life.
You have a lot of gas.
You've been craving pickles and starches.
You suddenly crave lemons.
You are fatigued and sleepy.
Your feet are swollen all the time.
You would rather eat vegetables than anything else.
You still have a pleasant outlook on life.
You are suddenly interested in sports.
Your hair is longer and thicker.

You Must Be Having a Girl Because...

Your girl has stolen your beauty and you've lost your looks.
You are carrying the baby low.
Men are very attracted to you.
You lose your appetite from time to time.
You have experienced a lot of nausea.
You have been craving meats instead of grains.
Your sweet tooth is never satisfied.
Your face is pudgy and your nose takes up half your face.
Your hips are spreading at a rapid rate.
You have regular bouts of moodiness.
You are cooking and cleaning more than ever.
Your hair is breaking off and it's flat, brittle, and dry.

Blue Is Not Just for Boys

 hawnese from Richmond, Virginia, couldn't wait to get the results of her sonogram. As soon as she found out she was having a boy, the Mama-to-be went on a major shopping spree.

She bought light blue onesies, dark blue socks, blue-and-white-striped sweaters, and all kinds of denim clothing covered with trucks, boats, balls, and things that little boys love.

When it came time to decorate the nursery, Shawnese went equally nuts. She stocked his room with toys and hung pictures of cute little black boys. A sign on the door read "Welcome to Ryan's Room," and his name was proudly spelled out in giant dark blue fabric letters just over his crib.

There was just *one* problem. On the day baby Ryan came into the world, *he* just happened to be a *she*. Shawnese was shocked! She never thought the sonogram results could be WRONG. All that hard work and planning and Shawnese had a sweet little girl. Shawnese liked the name so much that she still called her daughter Ryan. And though she didn't bother to return the baby's blue wardrobe, she did add touches of pink and yellow flowers to brighten the room.

Ask Ryan today what her favorite color is and she'll tell you *blue*. "I even like blue lollipops," Ryan says, smiling ear to ear. And even if she's dressed in blue from head to toe, as her face lights up and her eyes twinkle, there is no question that little Ryan is a girl through and through.

Ms. Coleman, It's a Boy!

Oooh, no! I didn't want to believe it, but Dr. Hurst confirmed the sonogram results. My heart had been set on having a little girl, but the blurry black-and-white picture—on which, by the way, I couldn't figure out where the head or body was positioned without help—was proof that my unborn child was a little boy.

Sure, I was happy that my baby was healthy. But, in a flash, my smile faded and tears rolled down my chubby cheeks. I was horrified about the challenge that was before me—raising a black boy. Of course, the world will be kind to baby Jordan (I had already selected a girl's name and a boy's name), but what will happen to my son when he becomes a teenager and then a black man?

Will the same white folks who cuddle baby Jordan and pinch his cheeks still think he's adorable when he's a teenager—possibly wearing whatever hip-hop, cool kid style that's fashionable—and resembling every police sketch issued across the nation?

Historically, this country hasn't treated black men with the same respect as their white counterparts. What do I tell Jordan when he realizes that his teachers may not have the same expectations for him as they do for his little white classmates, or if he decks someone for calling him nigger, or if a little old white lady holds her purse extra tight because my son has stepped onto an elevator? What do I tell him if he graduates from college at the top of his class and still can't enjoy the good life without constantly being reminded that he is black, or if he is dressed in a business suit and still can't hail a cab in Manhattan because some cabby thinks he looks threatening? What do I tell my precious son?

It was a heart-wrenching moment for me—a single, African-American mother. Which brought another issue to light—my marital status. That in itself could also affect the way some people choose to deal with my child. What will I tell Jordan when he wants to know why his daddy doesn't live with us?

Damn! I couldn't stop the tears. My mind became consumed with even more terrible thoughts—like gang violence, police brutality, drugs, and jail—the same fearful thoughts that African-American mothers have had for generations.

I cried all the way home. I called Mama and told her that she would soon have a grandson. She was happy and didn't understand my tears. After expressing my feelings, she explained that my job as a mother was to give my son lots of love, understanding, and nurturing.

"Always be a role model," Mama said. "Introduce your son to God, teach him right from wrong, get involved with his education and social activities, keep up with who he hangs out with, and never let him get too big for his britches."

I can always count on Mama to calm my fears, but just as I was finally cooling off, she scolded me. "Now get yourself together and don't let me hear you crying again. The baby has feelings, too, and he will think you don't like him," Mama said. "Just thank God that your son is healthy."

When I hung up the telephone, I looked in the mirror and forced a smile. Instead of worrying about all the negative stereotypes that exist for little black boys, I thought about all the positive black men—like my dad, my Uncle Gene, and my minister, the Reverend Gregory Jackson—who Jordan would be able to see on a regular basis.

I thought about all the courageous black men in history who did not allow inequality, discrimination, or the color of their skin to put a damper on their dreams. I thought about all the black men I know who are doctors, lawyers, ministers, engineers, politicians, entrepreneurs, civic leaders, police officers, professional athletes, corporate executives—hardworking and productive citizens. Then, my smile appeared naturally. The truth of the matter is that my son is African-American royalty with every opportunity to do the right thing, and I know that with God's blessings, my love and guidance, Jordan will do just fine.

Words of Truth, Love, and Encouragement for My African-American Prince

My son, my love, my African-American Prince,
never teeter-totter on both sides of any fence.

Make wise decisions, then stand firm and tall,
never look back, don't waver or fall.

Mama will help you as much as she can,
but God will help you become a strong black man.

The challenges facing black boys are serious today,
don't let racism, prejudice, or bigotry stand in your way.

Even with credentials you may run into a dead end,
never let it break your spirit, just lean on a friend.

Some days you can't hail a cab or get the job interview,
don't give up, my prince, it's not a reflection of you.

All black Mamas must tell their son,
of Shaka, Frederick, W.E.B., Booker T., Marcus, Medgar,
Martin, and Malcolm.

Benjamin, Adam, Thurgood, Langston, and Ulysses Kay,
you could go down in history like them some day.

You may be judged by your hairdo or color of your skin,
by the same kind of people who enslaved
and lynched your kin.

Don't become consumed by people of this kind,
respect, honor, and befriend those who value your mind.

Mama will arm you with knowledge of
the present and past,
be cautious of vanilla candy and cops who harass.

There's Emmet Till, Rodney King, and, of course, O.J.,
each took a fall and made news in their day.

Keep hope alive, that's what Rev. Jesse Jackson has to say,
steady your eyes on the prize if you want a brighter day.

I cannot prepare you for what's ahead in life,
a solid education, love, respect, and then a good wife.

Start a family of your own, then pass my words on,
sharing "My African-American Prince," long after I'm gone.

My son, my love, my African-American Prince,
in the future, Mama's words will make much more sense.

Always strive to be the best you can be,
and remember you come from deep chocolate royalty.

An impressive culture—rich, wise, and bold,
Be proud of your African heritage as you grow old.

God Bless You, My African-American Prince!
Love Ya, Mama

Words of Wisdom for Raising an African-American Boy

We have to stop spoiling our sons and raising our daughters. Little boys should be required to cook and clean just like girls. If we do too much for our sons, they will not make good husbands.

Jacqueline, Seattle, Washington

In the long run, boys stay close to Mama. Sure they eventually take a wife, but you'll be his favorite girl for life.

Mae, Orlando, Florida

Spare the rod, spoil the child—that's what the Bible says. I agree wholeheartedly, because in this day and age, if you don't discipline your son, the cops will do it for you.

Sharita, Roxbury, Massachusetts

Boys are less work in the long run. Most boys love and respect their Mama—seldom do you hear about them talking back or sassing Mama.

Bonita, Las Vegas, Nevada

Make sure your son can read and write. There's a man on our block who has been dreaming about playing in the NBA since high school. He played with my sons and he'll probably play with my grandsons too. Sure, all the boys respect him on the court, but that doesn't count for much. I encouraged my sons to earn respect in the classroom. Sure, their game is a bit rusty, but their mind isn't.

Lula, Brooklyn, New York

Words of Wisdom for Raising an African-American Girl

Let's get our daughters out of the bedrooms and kitchens and get them into the boardrooms. We should encourage them to be independent and self-sufficient.

Dorothy, Bronx, New York

When my girls became teenagers, I warned them that their reputation was all they had in this world and it was up to them to preserve it. A good reputation goes a long way for a young lady.

Buellah, Oakland, California

Don't shelter your little girl, let her live and learn. If you teach her to always do right, you don't have to worry about her doing wrong.

Cathy, Roxbury, Massachusetts

I tell my daughter that it is not very ladylike to spit, swear, or speak too loudly. I tell her there are other ways to be noticed if that's what she's searching for.

Peaches, Chicago, Illinois

My baby girl is forty-three years old and I am still telling her the same thing that I told her when she was a little girl . . . trust in the Lord and everything will work out just fine. I think that's the best advice anyone can give their little girl.

Emogene, Washington, D.C.

chapter five

mama's dos and don'ts

You Better Watch Out, You Better Not Pout; It Just Might Affect How Your Baby Comes Out

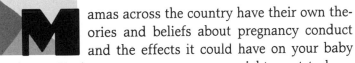

Mamas across the country have their own theories and beliefs about pregnancy conduct and the effects it could have on your baby and you. During your pregnancy, you might want to keep these things in mind.

- If you use profanity, your baby will be baldheaded.

- If you visit too many sick people, your baby will be deformed.

- If you imitate someone's voice, your baby will sound like that person when he cries.

- If you let a pregnant woman comb your hair, your hair will fall out.

- If you sleep all day, your baby will be lazy.

- If you stay up late at night, your baby will never sleep.

- If you are happy, your baby will be cheerful and outgoing.

- If you sleep on your stomach, your baby will have a flat nose.

- If you reach up above your head, you risk the chance of the umbilical cord wrapping round your baby's neck and choking him. In Jamaica, Mamas-to-be also believe that crocheting or walking under a fence may choke the baby.

- If you tie a string around your waist, it will prevent the baby from moving a lot.

- If two pregnant women walk down the street together, one will give birth to a stillborn.

If You Tease or Mimic a Handicapped Person While You're Pregnant, Your Baby Will Suffer the Same Handicap

Rheana, a native New Yorker, never believed in old wives' tales. When she was pregnant, Rheana made fun of a man who lived in town who walked with a limp. She tried to describe the guy to her friends, but it wasn't until she imitated him and started limping around the room that her friends figured out who she was talking about.

Rheana's impersonation was so good that everyone busted out laughing. She loved the attention and kept the girls in stitches at the poor guy's expense.

"You shouldn't mimic that man while you're pregnant," one friend warned.

"Yeah," another chimed in, "your baby will end up limping just like him. Didn't your Mama ever tell you that if you tease or mimic a handicapped person when you're pregnant, your baby will end up just like that person?"

Rheana just laughed and never thought twice about it. Until, that is, three months later, when she delivered a baby with one leg significantly shorter than the other. The doctors had no medical theories to explain why her daughter's leg was shorter—but they told her that her poor daughter would walk with a limp the rest of her life.

Rheana was completely guilt-stricken and the words of her friends came back to haunt her. She suddenly became a believer and vowed never to tease or poke fun at anyone else, whether she was pregnant or not.

If You Go to Funerals When You're Pregnant, Your Baby Will Be Born with Supernatural Powers

long time ago, in Rocky Mountain, North Carolina, there was an elderly woman named Miss Essie whose granddaughter, Edna, had just lost her godmother and wanted to pay her respects at the funeral. But Edna was pregnant with twins, and Miss Essie warned her that pregnant women should not go to funerals or else their baby may be born with supernatural powers.

"My friend Annie went to a funeral when she was expecting, and her baby girl ended up playing with nothing but imaginary friends," Miss Essie said. "And you remember Mertha? Same thing happened to her son. Po' boy ended up in the loony bin."

The young mother said she was tired of hearing all the pregnancy myths and stories from the past, and grabbed her coat and headed for the church. Yet, as she walked through the doors of the church, a silver-haired deaconess stopped Edna. She advised her to sign the book and leave.

"Don't you know pregnant women should *not* attend funerals?" the deaconess said. "For the sake of your baby, please go."

But Edna *had* to pay her respects and she headed for the casket. She viewed the body of the elderly woman and gently touched her face. Edna remembered the good old days and was quite upset the woman would never see her twin babies. Edna walked away from the casket and sat in the church.

One month later, the twins were born, each with a thick white mucous coating on their tiny faces. Edna's GrandMa immediately panicked.

"Babies born with veils will see ghosts and connect with spirits," Essie said. "See, I told you not to go to the funeral."

Edna's doctor explained that *all* babies were born with a coating, but the doctor did admit that the twins' coating was extremely thick and hard to rinse off.

But despite the grandmother's concerns, the babies were very alert and cheerful. They rarely cried or made a fuss. In fact, the babies were so mild-mannered that Edna's grandmother was convinced they were not normal—she said it was just a matter of time before they started talking to ghosts.

Although Miss Essie was usually right about everything, she was very wrong about her great-grandchildren. You see, Edna's babies turned out to be just fine. So, as far as Edna could tell, it was just another old superstition and Mamas-to-be should feel free to pay their respect to loved ones who have passed on.

Don't Talk Badly About Ugly People While You're Pregnant or Else Your Child Will Look Just Like That Person

ophie was a gorgeous girl from Bermuda—the standard of beauty for the 1920s, and then some. She had thick, wavy black hair, almond eyes, and a toffee complexion inherited from her mother—the kind of beauty that won her the adulation of everyone on her Caribbean island, and even a few modeling jobs here and there.

The only problem was that Sophie knew she was gorgeous and had little tolerance for those less fortunate than she.

Naturally, Sophie expected that her good looks would automatically filter to all of her children. After all, her first child, Barbara, was just as beautiful as she—and so she assumed this baby would be just as adorable.

But, unfortunately, it was not to be for her second child—and Sophie had no one to blame but herself.

During Sophie's pregnancy, an insurance man came knocking at her door. The poor man had a face that was completely distorted—his eyes were much too close together and his mouth twisted oddly to the right side. Sophie couldn't help herself. She took one look at the guy, broke down in laughter, and left the room.

When the salesman left, Sophie got a scolding from her mother: "You should not poke fun at people, especially not in your condition," her mother chastised. "My grandmother always told me that if you talk meanly about ugly people while you're pregnant, your child will end up looking just like that person."

"Oh, please!" Sophie said in exasperation. "Surely that's just an old wives' tale."

"You should beg God to forgive you," the mother warned. "I'm very serious."

Despite pleading from her mother, Sophie refused to apologize to the man. Instead, she took it a bit further by telling all her friends about the man's distorted features. She went so far as to imitate him by using her fingers to show how badly the man's face was twisted.

Well, Sophie learned her lesson in a big way. A few months later, Sophie gave birth to a baby boy with ten fingers, ten toes, two eyes entirely too close together, and a mouth twisted to the right side! He had all the features of the man who Sophie so cruelly mocked.

Blinded by love for her little bundle of joy, Sophie didn't realize what had happened. But other people did. Joc-Joe's twisted mouth and close eyes were not easy to miss. And just as Sophie laughed at the salesman, Joe-Joe's classmates laughed at him. They would send him home in tears almost every day. Sophie still could not understand.

But it all became painfully clear to Sophie when she was at the market one day with her beautiful daughter, Barbara.

Barbara pointed out the twisted face of the insurance man that Sophie had ridiculed years ago. "Look, Mama, look! That man looks just like Joe-Joe!"

Suddenly, it all came back to her. From that day on, Sophie always listened to her Mama, and never again did she speak badly of people—especially when she was pregnant.

If You Drool a Lot When You Are Pregnant, Your Baby Will Cut Teeth Early

rooling is a common problem for many pregnant women, and if you happen to suffer from this symptom, it means your baby will probably cut teeth early.

A woman named Arletha drooled so much during her pregnancy that she constantly kept a box of tissues with her. Months later, Arletha's baby girl was born with *two teeth* in her mouth. No one could believe it.

Now, I know it sounds a bit far-fetched, but I can personally back up this old wives' tale. Like Arletha, I drooled a lot when I was pregnant, and though my son wasn't born with any teeth, he did have eight teeth in his mouth by the time he was six months old! Nobody believed me until he opened his mouth and they could see for themselves.

Jordan's teeth were so big that he chomped up everything in sight—Mr. Goodbars, barbecued spareribs, and countless bits of paper—even at a very young age. My cousin nicknamed him "Choppy-Choppy"—and, to this day, when I hear a pregnant woman complaining about drooling, I tell her my tale.

Pregnancy and Animals

There is an old wives' tale rooted in African-American history that pregnant women should not come in close contact with animals.

The family cat may be cute and cuddly, but keep him away from your newborn baby. Many women of color believe that cats will take the baby's breath away and steal all the oxygen the baby needs to survive.

And while a furry little rabbit's foot may bring you luck at the slot machines in Las Vegas or Atlantic City, some women advise Mamas-to-be to put it away while you're pregnant, just to play it safe. There's a chance your baby could end up with big, floppy ears like Roger or buckteeth like Bugs, so don't try your luck. Just leave your rabbit's foot in the drawer until baby is born. You see, pregnant women fear that if they come in contact with an animal, the features may rub off on baby.

Jodi, for example, a young girl who grew up in Richmond, Virginia, in the 1940s, was warned not to look at dogs and rub her stomach at the same time or else her child would come out looking like that dog.

"I don't know if it's true or not, but I didn't take any chances," said Jodi, a Mama of five. "There is no evidence to prove or disprove it, but every time I became pregnant I stayed far away from dogs."

Here are some more animal tales that pregnant women shared with me:

- ◆ If you come in contact with a snake, your baby will have rough skin.

- ◆ If you stare at a monkey, your baby will scratch all the time.

- ◆ If you get sprayed by a skunk, your baby's bowel movements will have a terrible odor.

- ◆ If you come face-to-face with a bear, your baby will be hairy.

- ◆ If you pet a pig, your baby will be baldheaded and plump.

- ◆ If you trap a mouse, your baby will squeak when he talks.

- ◆ If you come in contact with a sheep, your baby will have nappy hair.

chapter six

remedies and cure-alls for mamas-to-be

Okay, nobody said you would feel your best during pregnancy. Every Mama at some point during her pregnancy will suffer some kind of discomfort or pain. Lucky for you, most of these conditions are temporary, and Mamas across the world have provided these down-home remedies and cure-alls that just may make you feel better.

Ankles and Feet (Swelling and Soreness)

Soak feet in warm water and Epsom salts.

Massage feet with warm lotions and creams.

Elevate feet as much as possible.

Wear loose-fitting shoes that allow feet to breathe.

   (If your feet seem to be getter bigger, they probably are. Chances are they will remain that size, so don't even think about squeezing them back into those size nine Via Spiga mules 'cause your heel will hang out.)

Avoid eating salty foods.

Backache

Kick off the high heels, mules, and sling-backs and pull out the flats and sneakers.

Sleep on a firm mattress to relieve some of the pain.

Breasts (Swelling and Soreness)

Place cold leaves of cabbage or collard greens in your bra
to relieve the pain. (My cousin Erika's mother-in-law
recommended this one. She swears it worked for her!)
After making a cup of tea, put the warm tea bag in your bra.
Massage breasts with ice cubes.
Place a cold cloth over breasts.
Always wear a bra when breasts are sore.

Constipation

Eat a lot of prunes, raisins, and high-fiber foods.
Drink at least eight glasses of water a day.

Heartburn

Heartburn during pregnancy is very common. Not every
woman suffers from it, but if you are one of the unlucky
ones who do, here are some pointers to help you cure it:

Eat slowly—chew each mouthful at least ten times before
you swallow.
Drink a cup of hot water combined with a teaspoon of
honey and vinegar. The hotter the water, the better this
works.
Cut back on eating fried foods.
Combine a teaspoon of ginger with a cup of warm water
and drink it.

And, by the way, for all you Mamas-to-be who are suffering from heartburn, you may be curious to know that
there is an old wives' tale that claims heartburn means your
baby will have a headful of hair. . . .

Heartburn and Hair Go Hand in Hand

When Pam Warner was pregnant with her son, actor Malcolm-Jamal Warner, who climbed to celebrity status with his starring role as Theo Huxtable on *The Cosby Show,* she suffered terribly from heartburn. Pam said she tried everything to cure it, but nothing seemed to give her the relief she needed.

Each time Pam complained, the women in her family told her that her constant indigestion was a surefire indication that her child would be born with a lot of hair.

What one had to do with the other was a mystery to Pam, but she listened intently to the womanly advice. Though Pam had her doubts, in the end the women were right.

"Malcolm was born with a full head of hair," Pam remembered. "The amount of hair he had was unbelievable."

My friend Beverly can back this up. She, too, suffered badly from heartburn and she, too, had a baby with a full head of hair.

"My daughter had so much hair, I thought I had given birth to boxing promoter Don King," Beverly joked. "It was sticking up and looking crazy and there was nothing I could do to help my little sweetie."

Hemorrhoids

While some women told me that fresh fruit and a lot of juice helps to relieve the itching and discomfort, I found that a warm bath with Epsom salts did the trick for me. Either way, the good news is, hemorrhoids don't usually last long.

Itchy Skin

Using lotion provides temporary relief, but wearing loose-fitting clothes makes a big difference, too. If the elastic in your underwear or pants is tight, put that clothing away until your pregnancy is over.

Mood Swings

Your hormones are on vacation and going crazy, so your best bet is to keep the communication lines open with your mate, family, and friends to avoid depression. When you're pregnant, you can be happy one moment and sad the next—this is normal—and there is no known cure. The best comfort will come from your loved ones who understand what you're going through.

Morning Sickness

Morning sickness is one of the most common symptoms associated with pregnancy, but if you ask me, the term is misleading. Nausea sneaks up on Mamas-to-be *any* time of the day, not just in the mornings and usually at the most inconvenient times.

What can be said? It's just a part of pregnancy for many women and the darnedest things can set it off. Although yours truly had only a few small bouts with nausea, I remember each episode as if it were yesterday. Yet, lucky for me, my cousin Angelita gave me just the cure!

In my fifth month of pregnancy, I grabbed a cab in Manhattan to meet Angelita. We were going to see a play, and by the time the cab dropped me off, I was feeling extremely nauseous. I had broken into a cold sweat and my stomach churned as if I had food poisoning. Everything seemed to be spinning. Angelita, a mother herself, took one look at me and knew I was not well.

"Don't worry, Chris," she said, putting her arm around me. "I've got just the cure. What you need is a bag of potato chips."

We walked around the corner and bought a bag of chips. Angelita swore that the salt from the chips would settle my stomach. At the time, I was desperate for a cure. I would have agreed to almost anything and I started munching. Within minutes I felt better. Sure enough, Angelita was right! She said her Mama had shared the potato chip remedy with her when she was pregnant. From that day on, until my son was born, I walked around with a small bag of potato chips in my purse, and it saved me on many occasions.

My final spell of nausea was particularly humorous. I was at the beauty parlor one Saturday morning, and my beautician, Santa, was rolling up my hair with curlers the size of soda cans. It was extremely hot that day, darn near 95 degrees, and the air conditioner was not all that powerful. A man in his late forties walked to the front of the shop, where I was sitting. He had a gazillion tiny pink rollers in his head. After he walked past me, I became queasy. The smell of rotten eggs lingered in the air.

My beautician sensed my discomfort and asked me what was wrong.

"I smell something awful and it's making me sick," I whispered to her.

"Oooh, it is probably his Jheri curl," Santa said, pointing to the man with the tiny pink curlers.

The next five minutes crawled by. I felt sicker and sicker. Between the Jheri curl odor and the sweltering heat, I thought I would have to be hospitalized. Unable to stand it another second, I shouted: "That Jheri curl is making me sick! Please open the door or get me away from him! Please!"

Santa rushed over to open the door and I ran out. The man with the Jheri curl was ushered to the back of the shop. The fresh air did wonders, but it was my trusty bag of potato chips that truly saved the day.

Almost every Mama I know has complained to me about nausea, and though I swear by the bag of potato chips, I've compiled this list of cure-alls from Mamas I spoke with. . . .

Remedies for Morning Sickness and Nausea

Sit down and put your head between your legs.
Suck on a lemon.
Eat salty snacks like chips, saltine crackers, and pretzels.
Drink a glass of warm ginger ale, cola, or club soda.
Eat well-seasoned fried chicken skin.
Sprinkle a little bit of salt on your tongue.
Lie down and try to go to sleep.
Sit in a dark, air-conditioned room.
Chew a stick of gum.
Eat a slice of dry toast.
Suck on a piece of peppermint or rock candy.

Also, you should know that extreme nausea could very well mean that you've got not one but *two* buns in the oven. Take my friend Leslie, for example. . . .

Nausea Could Mean Double Trouble—TWINS!

eslie was so sick during her first trimester that she lost eleven pounds. She had morning sickness around the clock and spent more time in the ladies' room than she did at her desk. Leslie's condition had gotten so bad that she carried a brown paper bag at all times, just in case she couldn't make it to the bathroom.

This did not take her female relatives by surprise. In fact, there were several women in Leslie's family who had experienced the same kind of nausea during pregnancy. Each of them gave birth to twins.

"You must be having twins," Leslie's Mama said. "Only twins make you this sick. Your Aunt Laverne was sick as a dog when she was pregnant with your cousins. And my Mama was terribly sick when she was pregnant with me and my twin brother."

"Twins do run in our family," Leslie replied, before dashing out of the room and into the bathroom. When she returned, her Mama had made her a warm cup of tea.

A week later, Leslie went to the doctor for a checkup and a sonogram. Sure enough, there were two heartbeats, two heads, and two of everything else. Leslie was indeed pregnant with twins. So if you are suffering from extreme bouts of nausea, I'd suggest visiting your doctor. You just may have two little darlings on their way.

Muscle Cramps

Take a warm bubble bath and add a little Epsom salts.
Place a heating pad on the cramping area of your body.
Massage the area for at least ten minutes.

Shortness of Breath

Gasping for air and shortness of breath are very common
during the last month of pregnancy because the baby is
pushing on your lungs. Climbing the stairs or tying your
shoe could actually wear you out—even the simplest tasks
can be exhausting. So my advice to you is to take it easy.
After the baby drops, you will get quick relief.

Stretch Marks

Another unpleasant symptom of pregnancy is stretch
marks—but thanks to our ancestors, there is hope. Pregnant slave women used to religiously rub down their stomachs, buttocks, breasts, thighs, and upper arms with globs
of lard to prevent stretch marks. The slaves received the
lard every Saturday from their slave owners as part of their
weekly food ration, but Mamas-to-be were more interested
in preserving their bellies than feeding them, so they
rubbed much of the lard on their skin hoping to keep it
tight and beautiful.

This remedy has been passed on throughout the generations, and though every woman I've spoken to seems to
have her own version, almost all of them swear that their
concoction worked for them.

A woman I met in Baltimore named Lynetta said her
Mama and aunts from South Carolina used to rub cooking

oil on their stomachs. Lynetta thought her Mama was exaggerating, so she called her Aunt Bertha in Sumter. "That's right," Aunt Bertha said. "None of the women in our family got stretch marks. We owe it all to our great-great-aunt Sadie—a slave who started the family tradition."

Then there was Hazel, from Charleston, West Virginia, who said she is stretch-mark-free thanks to a homemade concoction of baby oil, Vaseline, aloe vera sap, and lemon juice that was handed down from her Mama and grand-Mama. Hazel doesn't have an exact recipe, but shares that just a dab of each all mixed together does the trick.

If you don't want to be bothered making concoctions, Lisa from Washington, D.C., said a jar of Mother's Friend— a cream that she bought at a local drugstore—kept the squiggle lines off her tummy. If you're wondering what the best or the most effective concoction is, I honestly don't know. However, after hearing about every home remedy from here to Nigeria, I came up with my own ritual. One night I would rub cocoa butter on my stomach, the next night some vitamin E oil, and finally Keri lotion. Every third night I'd start the process all over again, determined to avoid those unsightly lines.

My Mama said it doesn't matter what the concoction; she just claimed lubrication would relax the skin and prevent the stretch marks.

Turns out Mama was right. Not only do my friends swear by it but it actually worked for me. I only have three barely visible stretch marks on each side of my stomach—which means I could possibly wear a bikini, if I could only lose some weight.

PART TWO

labor and
delivery

Hold on, you're almost there! It shouldn't be much longer before you're feeling the baby make his or her way out of your womb and into the world. Scary? Exciting? I know. But <u>oooh</u> the joy of holding your baby for the first time—that's all the encouragement you'll need to get you through. Be strong! Rejoice! <u>You are woman, hear you roar!</u>

chapter seven

due dates

Remember when Mamas were told only which month to expect their baby? Nowadays, doctors predict the *exact* due date at the first prenatal visit. And if the Mama doesn't deliver within two weeks of that set due date, doctors will often induce labor.

Even with today's modern medicine, most Mamas are ready to deliver by that last month and will try anything to encourage the baby to be born. Here are some tips:

- Pam said a long walk in the park helped her go into labor. But don't go too far from home.
- Bobbi said a hot cup of chicken broth laced with black pepper brought on her labor.
- My cousin Karen ate an extralarge salami-and-ham hero sandwich topped with jalapeño peppers hours before her contractions began.
- I recommend a thirty-two-ounce bottle of Pepsi. It worked for me.

While most Mamas said it was food that gave them the push, others relied on exercise, prayer, and meditation. But of all the stories I collected, singer CeCe Winans summed it up best.

"Only God knows the date and time," CeCe reminded me. Your little bundle of joy will make his entrance when the time is right. Be patient—your baby is a gift from God.

A Swig of Castor Oil in Your Last Days of Pregnancy Will Induce Labor

y friend Sissy was ready to deliver—just plain old tired of being pregnant. She was nine days past her due date and was ready to trade in her maternity clothing and pudgy body for her tailor-made dresses and prepregnancy shape. Well, her Mama-in-law had just the cure.

"Take some castor oil and the baby will come on down," she told Sissy matter-of-factly.

Sissy laughed at the idea, although her Mama-in-law was not the only one urging her to take a little castor oil—several of her Mama's friends had told Sissy the same thing.

"Just take a swig," one friend suggested. "It's been working for years. A lot of babies have entered this world with a little nudge from castor oil."

Sissy was tempted, but she wanted to give the baby time. She was a firm believer that the baby would come when the time was right, so she waited another day. But when her baby still hadn't arrived, Sissy gave in and gulped down a tablespoon of castor oil before bed—about five hours later, Sissy went into labor and delivered a beautiful baby girl.

chapter eight

labor pains

If you don't like hearing tales about labor and delivery, flip to the next story. But for those of you who like the whole truth, and nothing but the truth, read on.

Wear Onyx Jewelry into the Delivery Room to Lessen the Pain

o one said labor was going to be easy, but my great-aunt did advise my Mama to wear onyx jewelry to lessen the pain. She said that an onyx ring, necklace, or bracelet would help absorb excruciating pain. Though Mama didn't believe it, the story had been passed down to her from a family friend and so, on the way to the hospital, Mama grabbed her onyx ring from her jewelry box.

Unfortunately for Mama, she had a delivery from hell. The doctors had an extremely hard time trying to get me out because I was so big. "We need you to push," the doctor insisted. "You have to try harder."

Hours later, the doctors finally used forceps to pull me out. Needless to say, the onyx ring didn't do anything for

Mama's pain, but believe it or not, thirty-two years later, when I went into labor myself, Mama told me the same old wives' tale.

Although she was clear that it didn't work for her, Mama said that other women swore by it. With the first contraction, I immediately put on my onyx earrings, hoping it would work for me. Well, the first eight hours of labor were painless—I remember standing in my kitchen singing "I Am Woman, Hear Me Roar." The contractions felt like minor menstrual cramps, and I foolishly believed my onyx earrings were guiding me through the contractions.

But as time progressed, the contractions got worse and I began to feel like I was in the ring with Mike Tyson, getting beat over and over again. Suddenly, the onyx earrings seemed no match for the pain. Worse yet, when I arrived at the hospital, the nurse said I had only experienced Braxton Hicks', which were prelabor cramps and should not have been *that* painful.

When they rolled me into the delivery room, Jordan didn't want to come out at first. My doctor urged me to push harder, but after a while, I just couldn't. Mama and Jordan's dad were also by my side and did everything in their power to help me push, but to no avail. I was worn out—fit to be tied. Finally, the doctor used a suction device and, thankfully, out came Jordan.

As I lay stretched out on the table, still in pain, I promised to share the onyx old wives' tale just to prove that it didn't work, at least not for Mama and me. So, heed the warnings, and try this at your own risk.

A Rough Labor May Mean There Is Resentment Toward the Baby

Though doctors claim it's close to impossible to predict which women will have a difficult labor and which ones will not, black Mamas worldwide have their own theory. It has nothing to do with medical procedures; in fact, some Mamas claim it's all up to the baby.

For generations, women of color have believed that a long and painful labor is the direct result of a family member's ill feelings or resentment toward the baby. It's said that the unborn child can feel the negative energy while he is in the womb. Whether it's a Mama's worries about being a single mother, a father's concern about finances and paternity, or a sibling's jealousy toward the new arrival, the baby knows just what's going on.

So even though your water may break or you suffer from contractions and labor pains, the baby just might be doing everything possible to prolong his grand entrance into the world. Wondering what to do?

If your baby isn't ready to make his debut, try your best to be patient. No matter how much pain or discomfort you might be in, try to talk to your baby and reassure him that everything will be just fine. Once your baby knows he is loved and wanted, he'll come on out in no time.

No Pain, No Gain

amas have frequently been overheard telling their girlfriends about labor and delivery and how they dealt with the pain. For me, the contractions came fast and furious. The only relief came from an epidural.

The anesthesiologist gave me the needle, but it wore off long before Jordan actually made his arrival. I can remember pleading, without any semblance of shame, for another one of those miracle shots, like a street corner junkie in need of a fix. But despite my cries for help, Dr. Hurst refused to give me any more drugs.

"I need you to be able to push," Dr. Hurst said. "If you are numb, you will not be able to feel yourself pushing."

So much for modern medicine. Long before the epidural, Mamas-to-be were given potent painkillers, such as Demerol, which was administered to them intravenously. While it was believed that Demerol helped ease the pain, it tended to make Mamas sleepy, so they gradually stopped using it. Today, it is unheard-of, but some doctors even used to give Mamas-to-be tranquilizers to help them relax during the delivery.

My Aunt Hortense, a retired registered nurse who worked in her field forty-something years, remembers the days when doctors went so far as to place a mask over the Mama's nose and actually allowed her to inhale nitrous oxide, the very same anesthesia dentists once used. And before that, most women were given general anesthesia that put them to sleep while the doctors delivered their babies.

Though this method was painless for the Mama, it was no surprise when medical research later proved that painkillers and anesthesia sometimes adversely affected both the Mama and the baby.

That's why today's Mamas are given only the bare essentials. But, remember, no matter how bad you think it is, it is not nearly as bad as our ancestors had it. Slaves had no choice but to deliver babies without any painkillers at all. In fact, in African culture, some women believed that severe labor pains were connected to evil spirits, and in extreme cases, they feared a curse had been put on the Mama-to-be.

To get rid of the evil spell, female relatives would take a straw broom and sweep around the front door of the home for hours hoping to kill the spirits. Others forced the pregnant woman to drink strong herbal potions that were believed to frighten the evil spirits and force them to leave the woman's body. And a little old great-grandMa from Atlanta shared this secret. She said when she was pregnant, she drank a tin cup full of the strongest whiskey in the house and felt no pain at all.

Sorry, ladies, this probably won't go over big with your doctor, so my advice to you is to hold out for the epidural. And once the epidural wears off, you are on your own. No anesthesia, Demerol, or potent painkillers for today's Mamas—you've got to be strong!

Keep in mind that generations ago, Mamas did it all on their own. And, most of all, remember that the rewards you get from your baby can't compare to the pain. You'll find that your baby was worth it.

Walking and Exercise Will Prepare You for the Delivery Room

wenty-two-year-old Samantha was tickled pink that she was pregnant, but at the same time, she was dreadfully nervous about delivering the baby. She had heard one too many horror stories from her friends and now she simply feared the labor and delivery. She spoke to her doctor of her concerns, but he could offer no solid advice or surefire ways for an easy delivery. Yet, much to Samantha's relief, an old black woman who lived down the street told her that women who exercise regularly during pregnancy will have an easier delivery.

"Just think of the poor slave women who worked all day in the fields, and then had to endure labor without today's modern medicine. The reason they were so strong," she continued, "is because they kept themselves physically fit up until the day they delivered."

Well, that was all Samantha needed to hear. She turned into an exercise fanatic overnight. She took an aerobics class every day up until her eighth month of pregnancy. She did jumping jacks, lifted weights, and walked miles and miles. When she began her eighth month, Samantha slowed down a bit, but she began walking around the mall for exercise.

All the women in Samantha's family insisted that exercise would not help when it came time to deliver the baby.

"Only the good Lord can help," her sister said.

Her best friend, who had had a baby the year before,

thought it would help keep her weight down, but also encouraged her to relax and save her energy for the baby.

Samantha paid her friends and relatives no mind and kept her legs moving as often as she could. So it was no surprise to anyone when her water broke while doing a lap at the mall one day. When she arrived at the hospital, the nurses examined her and she was fully dilated. Within ten minutes, her eleven-pound baby girl popped right out. Even the doctors couldn't believe it.

"They told me almost no one delivers a baby so effortlessly and so quickly," Samantha boasted.

When Samantha brought her new baby home, one of the first people she visited was the old wise woman from down the street who gave her such good advice.

"The doctors wouldn't come out and say whether exercising was the trick or not," Samantha told the gray-haired woman. "But I know in my heart and soul that it was my saving grace. Now, I tell everyone that if you want an easy delivery, put on your sweats and Just Do It!"

chapter nine

delivering baby

Times have changed, but the worries of Mamas-to-be remain the same. As excited as you are to have the baby, your concerns, fears, and anxieties are normal. But trust me, all your worries will soon be over and you'll be glowing with pride over your new little girl or boy.

Breech Babies

 very Mama I know feared her baby would be breech. What would happen if the baby wasn't born head first?

Luckily, today's physicians have a number of ways to deliver breech babies safely. Often times, doctors will massage the Mama's stomach, applying a little pressure in hopes of guiding the baby's head into the proper position. If this is not successful, the baby is usually born by way of a C-section. It is no longer a major threat to your baby if he winds up in the breech position.

Yet, years ago, black Mamas had a lot more to fear. It was widely believed that breech babies would be less intelligent than others because their knowledge would be locked in their toes—instead of their brain. Crazy as it may sound to modern Mamas, it was a curse said to have started back in the late 1800s.

So, don't worry if your baby winds up in the breech position, he or she is bound to be fine. And as far as this old wives' tale goes, I don't buy it—intelligence is genetic and has nothing to do with being born headfirst.

Showering After Delivery Will Make You a Coldhearted Mama

hile most Mamas can't wait to take a long, hot shower after the stress of delivery and birth, many old black Mamas warn their female relatives not to.

My Aunt Julie's grandMa, known as Ga-Mama, urged her *not* to take a shower after her daughter was born in 1962.

"They goin' try to getcha to take a shower, but don't do it," Ga-Mama warned. "Them hospital folk don't know nothin' 'bout us colored folks."

"But, Ga-Mama, a shower would feel so good, and, besides, the nurses come around and tell you to take a shower," Aunt Julie argued.

"I don't care what those nurses say," Ga-Mama said. "Water will put cold in your body, and your baby needs the warmth of her Mama. The shower will chill you to the bone and make you a cold-natured Mama."

So when the nurses came around to give Aunt Julie a shower, she removed her gown, went into the bathroom, ran the water, and hoped the nurses wouldn't catch her.

"I pretended to take a shower because Ga-Mama said that once cold got into your body, it never left. You would be old before your time," Aunt Julie explained.

Aunt Julie is grateful to Ga-Mama, and now she gives

pregnant women the same advice. Aunt Julie gave the same advice to me after I delivered, but I told her that I'd pass. Sorry, but I couldn't wait to shower. Now, only time will tell if I'll be a coldhearted Mama.

Don't Wash Your Hair

In the early 1900s, Mamas were also warned not to wash their hair for six months after giving birth because their pores would be left open and they'd catch pneumonia and possibly die. Sounds ridiculous to us, but women took it to heart. One woman didn't wash her hair with water for twenty-five years! She had her first baby in 1923 and her last baby in 1946 (she's the proud Mama of fourteen children), and during that time she only washed her hair with hot oil and wiped it out. Believe it or not, she is still a picture of health and lives in North Carolina.

chapter ten

midwifery

Don't call me no doctor, don't call no nurse;
just call the granny woman with the big black purse.

Back in the days when doctors were few;
it was the midwife who helped pregnant women
get through.

Labor and delivery—she had no fear;
the skills of a doctor with more love and care.

The midwife birthed babies and used prayer to heal;
self-educated and powerful, with a legacy that's real.

It began during slavery and continues through today;
Mamas-to-be want to connect with our ancestors
in every way.

idwifery can be traced back to slavery—a time when the midwife—or granny woman, as she was affectionately called—delivered the babies of slaves and slave masters. When a woman thought she was pregnant, she would go to the midwife, who would confirm the pregnancy through massages and a breast examination.

Midwives were said to have the expertise and knowledge of ob-gyns. Yet, delivering babies was not their only function. Slave Mamas also believed midwives had healing powers and could cure sick babies and children through prayer. Whether they could really heal through prayer or not is uncertain, but it gave Mamas the faith, strength, and courage to believe their babies would lead strong and healthy lives.

Mirror, Mirror, on the Wall

eatrice exercised, ate healthy, meditated, and prayed daily for an easy delivery. When the midwife arrived at her Mississippi farmhouse, her looks startled Beatrice. It was not the same woman who had diagnosed Beatrice's pregnancy.

The midwife who initially examined Beatrice was young and beautiful, but the woman who showed up to deliver her baby was a bit older and extremely hard to look at. Her skin appeared to be burnt and her features were distorted.

When Beatrice's Mama arrived at the farm to assist the midwife with the delivery, she, too, was surprised to see such an ugly midwife. In fact, she purposely advised Beatrice to make sure her midwife was easy on the eyes because her appearance would play a major role in the delivery.

"If the baby sees an ugly midwife, he will not want to come out," Beatrice's Mama warned.

"Oooh, Mama," Beatrice replied. "I don't believe I have anything to worry about. I agreed to look for an attractive woman to deliver my baby just to satisfy you, not because I believed in it."

"Suit yourself, Beatrice," her Mama said. "But if I were you, I would try to find out what happened to the other woman."

As the labor pains increased, Beatrice couldn't care less who delivered the baby—she just wanted to get it over with. Several hours passed by and Beatrice still hadn't delivered. The baby's head peeked out each time she pushed, but the rest of the baby's body wouldn't budge. The midwife turned Beatrice on her side, applied pressure to her stomach, and did everything in her power to make Beatrice comfortable.

"I've been having a real hard time delivering babies here lately," the midwife admitted. "I can't imagine what's going on."

Beatrice's Mama raised her right eyebrow and puckered her lips. She wanted to tell the midwife that she was probably scaring the babies back into the womb, but she held her tongue.

The midwife told Beatrice to keep pushing. She pushed and pushed, but still no baby. Beatrice's Mama had remained quiet long enough. She politely asked the midwife to leave the room and within minutes Beatrice gave one good push and the baby miraculously popped out right into his grandMa's arms. Beatrice was in shock. She didn't really know if it was a coincidence or if the old wives' tale was indeed true, but from that day forward, she followed all of her Mama's advice.

It's All in the Black Bag

ack in the early 1930s, there was a little girl named Alameta who desperately wanted to know where babies came from. And despite the abundance of midwives who always came to deliver babies, no one would tell Alameta the truth. You see, in those days, children weren't taught very much about "grown folk stuff," like sex or babies.

In fact, Alameta's Mama told her storks were responsible for the birth of all babies. That's right, the stork! If a stork bit a woman on the leg, Mama claimed, she would become pregnant and the stork would return nine months later to deliver a baby boy or girl.

Yeah, right! Alameta thought—she never believed it. Uh-uhh, this little girl was too smart to fall for the stork theory.

"How would the stork know where to deliver each baby?" the seven-year-old girl asked. "And just where does the stork keep the babies before delivering them?"

Each time the midwife came down her street in Albany, Georgia, with her big black bag in hand, Alameta would ask: "Where's your stork? Is it in your black bag?"

"Ain't got no stork, chile," the silver-haired woman always answered.

Alameta continued her search for the truth about babies, but neither her Mama nor her aunts would entertain her inquiries. It was taboo for anyone to talk about sex, especially in the company of young children.

While sitting on her front porch one day and sharing a big glass jar of sweet water with her friends, Alameta told the other girls that she indeed knew where babies came from—and would tell them, too, if they could keep a secret.

Suddenly, all eyes were on Alameta and the girls huddled even closer around their friend.

"The midwife keeps the babies in her black bag until it's time for the delivery," she whispered. "But you can't tell anyone 'cause the grown-ups don't want us to know."

From that day forward, the little girls fell out laughing every time an adult told them that babies came from the stork. After all, their pal Alameta had set the record straight for them—at least that's what they believed for a long, long time.

Midwifery: More Than a Job, It's a Calling

ara Jean was a teenage girl from Richmond, Virginia, who grew up during the Depression and loved children. She was especially drawn to infants and loved them more than anything else in the whole world.

Sara Jean was also very interested in their journey into this world and read every book she could get her hands on about pregnancy, labor, and the miracle of birth.

Whenever someone in the family or neighborhood was pregnant, Sara Jean would spend hours on end with the Mama-to-be, rubbing her stomach and trying to predict what sex the baby would be.

She found her calling and dreamt of becoming a midwife, but her Mama had different plans for her daughter. You see, Sara Jean's Mama was afraid that her daughter's obsession with babies would influence her to become a teenage mother, like many of the other girls in Richmond. Her Mama wanted only the best for Sara Jean.

Sara Jean graduated from high school with honors and though she wanted nothing more than to become a midwife, she enrolled in college in North Carolina, at her Mama's insistence. But after only a few weeks, she dropped out and returned to Richmond. Sara Jean's Mama was heartbroken.

"Sara Jean, I want you to make something out of your life," her Mama pleaded. "Midwifery is like slave work. Black women today have much more opportunity. We should get away from jobs like that."

Her Mama's words really hit home, but Sara Jean still intended to become a midwife one day. She was grateful for the opportunity to attend college and graduated at the top of her class, receiving more teaching offers than any of her classmates.

Sara Jean's Mama was extremely proud of her daughter and encouraged her to return to Richmond. Sara Jean returned to Richmond, all right, but she had plans of her own. She hung her diploma on her Mama's living room wall, then had a heart-to-heart with her.

"Mama, I know you're going to be upset, but I have decided to take a job as a midwife," Sara Jean said. "I went back to school and got my teaching degree as you wished, and now I have to do something for me. Becoming a midwife is my calling."

Sara Jean's Mama embraced her daughter and shed a tear—she realized her pleas had fallen on deaf ears.

"Baby, you have my blessings. It's only fair that you are happy with your life and I know that this is your passion," her Mama said. "I'm just thankful you also have a solid education and a college degree. Be proud of yourself, chile, 'cause your Mama is sho' nuff proud of you."

Sara Jean and her Mama hugged and were at peace with one another. No surprise to anyone in her neighborhood, Sara Jean quickly became the most popular midwife in Richmond, Virginia, and was never happier in her life. She even put her teaching degree to work as she trained other women who were called to midwifery.

PART THREE

motherhood

Congratulations! Now you've entered the wonderful world of motherhood. Membership has its privileges. As you embark upon your new role as a Mama, you will find it incredibly rewarding, and at times incredibly overwhelming. But don't fret, I've compiled lots of advice from seasoned Mamas everywhere. So, celebrate, and have fun with your new bundle of joy!

chapter eleven

naming baby

Selecting the perfect name for your baby is one of the most important jobs a new Mama has. A baby's name is his or her first introduction to the world—as well as his permanent identity.

While some Mamas name their babies after relatives and friends, others use the Bible for guidance. Just think about all the Josephs, Joshuas, Timothys, Esthers, Marys, and Sarahs you know. But today's black Mamas are moving away from the more traditional names, and many are opting to give their newborns African names, like Nia, Imani, Hassan, and Hakim. All have a special meaning—and all are firmly rooted in African-American history and culture.

Just for the record, when I decided to name my son Jordan Christopher, it had nothing *at all* to do with Chicago Bulls' basketball star Michael Jordan—even though people ask me that question on a regular basis. If anything, I pray his life will be as tranquil as the river Jordan. And, more important, I wanted to give my son a power name that would one day help him get the interview, the job, the promotion, the partnership, and, yes, even the presidency—if that's his goal. Whatever your choice, just keep in mind your child has to live with his name for a lifetime—so, be kind.

African Names

*When the time comes around to give baby a name, some
mothers go for outrageous and others go for plain.*

*It seems like more and more black Mamas-to-be,
have decided to reach back into our African ancestry.*

*Instead of John, Tom, Joe, Debbie, or Maryanne,
today's Mamas are choosing names from the Motherland.*

*Hakim, Kesse, Tanisha, and Imani to name a few,
filled with spirit and love from our African heritage to you.*

*Afrocentric baby names are quite common today,
straight from Ghana, Nigeria, and, of course, Zimbabwe.*

*Each name has meaning for your little bundle of joy, here
are lists of African names for your baby girl and baby boy.*

Popular African Girl Names

1. Alike (Ah-lee-kee)—Lovely child (Nigeria)
2. Alile (Ah-lee-lee)—She weeps (Malawi)
3. Batini (Ba-tee-ne)—Innermost/deep thoughts (Swahili)
4. Dalila (Dah-lee-la)—Gentle (Swahili)
5. Dede (Deh-de)—First born girl (Ghana)
6. Fayola (Fah-yo-la)—Good luck (Nigeria: Yoruba)
7. Imani (Ee-ma-ni)—Faith (Swahili)
8. Keshia (Key-sha)—Favorite one
9. Nia (Nee-ya)—Purpose (Swahili)
10. Penda—Loved one (Swahili)
11. Rashida (Ra-shee-da)—Righteous one (Swahili)
12. Tanisha (Ta-nee-sha)—Born on Monday (Swahili)

Popular African Boy Names

1. Abasi (Aa-bass-ee)—Strict or stern (Swahili)
2. Akin (Ah-keen)—Brave (Nigeria: Yoruba)
3. Bem—Peace (Nigeria)
4. Daudi (Da-oo-de)—Beloved one (Swahili)
5. Garai (Gah-rah-ee)—Settled (Zimbabwe)
6. Gyasi (Ja-see)—Wonderful child (Ghana)
7. Hakim (Haa-kem)—Doctor (Ethiopia)
8. Jahi (Ja-hee)—Dignity (Swahili)
9. Kesse (Kee-se)—Fat newborn (Ashanti)
10. Kwame (Kwah-me)—Born on Saturday (Ghana)
11. Rudo (Roo-doh)—Love (Zimbabwe)
12. Uzoma—Born during a journey (Nigeria: Ibo)

Name Your Baby After Someone You Admire and Your Child Will Grow Up and Emulate That Person

ctress Irma Delores Hall, who played Aunt T—a blind, quick-lipped eighty-eight-year-old woman in the hit movie *A Family Thing*—was named after two people her mother most admired. The name Irma came from a family friend, a local schoolteacher who always touched the minds and hearts of students and their parents. Irma's middle name, Delores, was taken from the famous Hispanic actress Dolores Del Rio, the closest thing to looking like a black person on the silver screen. And you would be surprised how closely Irma Delores Hall emulated the two women.

Irma Hall taught high school in rural Texas for twenty-seven years and was greatly respected and admired, just like her namesake. Although Irma loved teaching, she secretly dreamed of one day becoming an actress, just like Dolores Del Rio, but never had time to pursue it. Yet, to her credit, at the ripe age of fiftysomething, Irma's dreams came true.

Movie director Raymond St. Jacques heard Irma reciting her poetry one day, and on a whim, he offered her a part in his 1973 movie *Book of Numbers*. Irma was a natural, and went on to perform in local theaters and a host of other movies. She retired from teaching in 1984 to focus exclusively on acting and became nearly as popular as Dolores Del Rio.

Everyone marveled at Irma's newfound fame and good luck. But Irma knows she had more than luck on her side.

"Some people say it's all in the genes." Irma laughs. "But I *know* it's all in the name."

Nicknames Are Anchored in Our Heritage

ne of the most important decisions a mother makes is what to name her baby, yet Mamas take this simple "luxury" for granted. During the days of slavery, many Mamas were denied the simple pleasure of naming their babies what they wanted.

On many plantations, the slave owner believed he had the right to name the children of his slaves because they were *his* property. Worse yet, families were constantly torn apart as slaves were sold, traded, and transferred from plantation to plantation on a whim. And since many of the slaves were denied their birth names, it made it almost impossible to locate family members later on in life.

But despite all these hardships, slaves did not allow it to break their spirit. Instead, many slave children were given nicknames that were used only by family members and only when the slave owner was not around. The nicknames were always personal, affectionate names that closely resembled the child.

Now that you know the history of nicknames, it may surprise you how many families are still calling relatives by nicknames. I can name ten off the top of my head and I'm sure you have kinfolk who still go by these names, too: there's Peanut, the littlest kid on the block; Monkey, who climbs on Mama's furniture; Sunny-Boy and Sunshine, who are always happy; and there's Boobie, Pooky, Li'l Mama, Big Man, Sister, Smiley—to name a few.

Now that you know the origin of nicknames, I hope you will appreciate them even more.

chapter twelve

bringing baby home

Now that you've given your little one a name, it's time to take him or her home and start your life together. I'm sure you've gotten your instructions from the doctor, but I think you'll find tips from these Mamas truly invaluable.

When my Mama was discharged from Hackensack Hospital in 1963, she was given a one-page sheet called "After Delivery Instructions." This sheet included the following information:

1. You may shower and wash your hair.
2. You should stay at home and do no work for the first week after your discharge from the hospital.
3. You may go up and down stairs once or twice daily, no more.
4. For every hour that you are up and about, spend one hour resting.
5. You may go out the second week if the weather is pleasant, once daily, and not for over two or three hours.
6. Sleep or lie on your abdomen for a while. This helps bring the womb back to normal position.

7. If your "bottom" is sore, or for cleansing purposes, a warm sitz bath is excellent.
8. Wear a bra. For painful breasts, you may apply an ice bag and also withhold salt and salty foods.
9. You may wear a girdle or a two-way stretch.
10. Continue with iron pill for three or four months.
11. Avoid all heavy lifting and heavy housework for six weeks.
12. No douching or intercourse until the baby is six weeks old.

When I delivered Jordan in 1995, the same hospital had expanded into the Hackensack Medical Center, and the one-page instruction sheet had been revamped into a twenty-eight-page booklet. It included a section on infant care with very specific instructions for everything from shampooing baby's hair to taking the baby's temperature.

While the 1963 instructions focused on the physical aftereffects of pregnancy, the modern-day version contained sections on postpartum and the emotional needs of the new mother. The hospital still recommended the sitz bath, but decreased the waiting period for sex to three weeks for C-section deliveries and "slightly longer" for vaginal births. Still, even with the updated, better, and bigger-than-ever instructions, I still came to rely on my relatives, friends, Jordan's nanny . . . and, of course, Mama, who always knows best.

Tips for New Mamas

very new Mama needs a few tips when it comes to caring for her infant and herself. While all the practical advice can be found in baby-care books, here's the real scoop from Mamas who have already *been there, done that!*

- ◆ Set visiting hours in your home for those who want to see the baby, because relatives and friends tend to be less considerate than they ought to be. This is especially true for those who do not have children and have absolutely no clue as to what you are going through. Put your foot down. Be assertive.

- ◆ Wear stockings and a pair of socks to keep your feet and legs warm. After you have a baby, your pores are open and the stockings and socks prevent cold from entering the body.

- ◆ Don't panic if you notice more hair on the floor when you're combing, many new Mamas lose an excessive amount of hair because of hormone imbalance.

- ◆ Your Mama might tell you to wait a month after delivery to take a bath because you can get an infection, but doctors say there's no need to fear. In fact, a few doctors said a warm bath would do wonders for a new Mama's stitches.

- ◆ Be sure to wear a lightweight girdle after delivery, especially if your baby is delivered by way of C-section. The tightness of the girdle will help contract your stomach muscles. I didn't listen and I am still thick around the middle.

◆ Get a friend to braid your hair or get a short cut in order to maximize your time. Hairdos that require a lot of fuss and bother slow new Mamas down.

◆ Gladly accept homemade meals that friends prepare because by the time you finish tending to your new baby, there will not be much time for cooking. In fact, some friends who are short on cash often give the Mama-to-be service coupons—promising to cook, clean, or baby-sit—that can be redeemed within a day's notice.

◆ The first bowel movement after having a baby is sometimes difficult. Mama says that prunes, raisins, or a hot plate of collard greens will help do the trick.

◆ Get a baby nurse, nanny, or ask a relative—one who has a lot of patience—to come spend the first week or two with you. First-time Mamas take a while to get used to being a Mama, which is often demanding and overwhelming.

◆ Never try to put your baby to sleep while lights are shining in your infant's face. The heat from the light will prevent her from dozing off.

◆ When the baby sleeps, be sure to go to sleep, too. It's impossible to nap at times when baby is still awake.

◆ Read a book to your newborn and sing songs to her on a regular basis to spark her creativity.

- Try to keep a diary, journal, photos, or videotapes of your baby's growth and development. Baby books and pictures will be fun to look at in years to come.

- Put your baby on a feeding and nap schedule as soon as possible. At the end of the day, put baby to sleep at the same time every night. Even as your baby goes into his toddler years, he will get sleepy at that time.

- It's okay to give baby a pacifier. In fact, most Mamas say it's easier to wean baby off a pacifier than a thumb.

- Don't be afraid to have a romantic evening after you get the okay from your doctor. Tending to the new baby is exhausting, but you'll be pleasantly surprised what a candlelight dinner and a tender night can do for you.

- And, last but not least, don't throw away your maternity clothes. You'll still need them when you come home. Greeting guests in nightgowns can be a bit awkward for you and your guests. And, hey, you never know when you'll have another one on the way.

chapter thirteen

feeding baby

To Breast-feed . . . or Not?

Another big decision for new Mamas is whether or not to breast-feed. There are pros and cons to each, so Mamas must carefully consider their options. Some Mamas may choose to breast-feed but find they can't. Not every new Mama produces enough milk to feed her baby.

Luckily, I was able to breast-feed my son, and I loved caressing Jordan and watching him pucker up for his vitamins and nutrients. I breast-fed for three and a half months—then Jordan cut his first two teeth.

While most doctors say that breast-feeding is the best and healthiest way to feed the baby, keep in mind that it is also very demanding and time-consuming because only you can supply the food. So when you make the choice, select the method that best fits your lifestyle and keep these tips in mind.

If you decide to breast-feed, make sure that you watch what you eat, because everything goes to the baby. So stay far away from gassy foods like cabbage, avoid spicy foods, and, most important, avoid alcoholic beverages.

Even if you decide to breast-feed, give your baby at least one bottle a day. It will be helpful when you want to leave her with a sitter.

Not Breast-feeding? Try Binding Your Breasts

omen who do not breast-feed are often bothered by the swelling of their breasts and want to drain the milk. Much like the tradition of body binding, women who do not breast-feed often bind their breasts, hoping the pressure will drain their milk.

Delores swears by this method. After delivering her daughter, she tightly wrapped towels around her breasts each day for eight weeks. Each day, she could see the milk saturating the towels. Delores said it was painless and very efficient.

"It also helped keep the breasts perky," Delores said. "Women who didn't bind, hung low."

Nursing Mamas Can't Get Pregnant

ack in the early 1920s, everyone told Mattie not to worry about birth control while she was nursing. They claimed it was impossible to get pregnant while breast-feeding and urged her to enjoy the freedom while she could.

No need to have condoms, creams, or pills—just enjoy the pleasures of making love. Mattie was told this so many times that she never bothered to check with her doctor.

Instead, she planned a romantic evening with her husband—a night to remember.

A month later, Mattie felt all the symptoms of pregnancy. The advice passed on by her friends was just an old wives' tale. Ooops! Guess that explains why Mildred's sister, Mabel, is only eleven months younger than she is.

Formulas and Concoctions

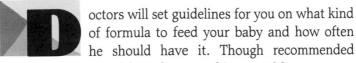octors will set guidelines for you on what kind of formula to feed your baby and how often he should have it. Though recommended dosages and types of formula vary a bit, most Mamas across the nation practice similar feeding practices. Yet, I was astounded to learn from black women of all ages from different parts of the world just how different baby formulas and feeding practices can be. Here are some of the more interesting ones. . . .

◆ When my Mama came home from the hospital with me in 1963, her doctor sent her home with a recipe for formula.

According to the instructions, she was supposed to mix six ounces of Carnation Evaporated Milk with fourteen ounces of water and two level teaspoons of Dextra Maltose #1.

She was told to divide the formula into six three-ounce bottles. Feeding times were set for 10:00 A.M., 2:00 P.M., 6:00 P.M., 10:00 P.M., 2:00 A.M., and 6:00 A.M.—but my Mama said I refused to stick to it. Instead, I wanted a little formula every two hours. So, like the good Mama that she was, she put the doctor's orders aside and fed me every two hours like I wanted. So, listen to your doctor's guidelines, but, remember, you and your baby will eventually fall into a schedule that works best for both of you.

◆ Carrie grew up in Warrenton, North Carolina, and her Mama used to feed her and her thirteen siblings a combi-

mama knows best

nation of boiled rice, sugar, and milk when they were babies. "We continued to eat it for breakfast as we got older," she said. "Rice was a breakfast food to us. I didn't know that people ate rice for dinner until I was an adult living in New York City."

◆ When there was no milk left in the house, some Mamas wrapped sugar in a cloth, dipped it in a bowl of water, and let their babies suck. This is called a "sugar tit" and though it dates back to slavery, it remains popular in the rural South to this day. Some Mamas believe this is how the pacifier originated.

◆ Delores Stewart said when she was a baby in the forties, her Mama used to feed her a combination of crumbled fish with rice and water.

◆ Hattie Anne said her Mama never breast-fed. Instead, she would boil a pot of water, add a few pinches of sugar, and crumble saltine crackers into the water.

◆ Before there was baby formula in the Dominican Republic, babies were either breast-fed or given a concoction made from cow's milk. Mamas would boil rice until it became thick and creamy, then add cow's milk and a bit of sugar. People said the combination would make the baby fat, but Dominican Mamas believed that a fat baby was a healthy baby.

◆ In Ethiopia, it's the Mamas-to-be, not the babies, who are given a special "concoction." When an Ethiopian woman announces that she is pregnant, family members and friends concoct a homemade pregnancy brew made from the juice of boiling oatmeal, lemon, and honey. It is rich in vitamins and minerals and extremely good for Mama and the baby. Once the drink is made, it is taken to the pregnant Mama's home and she is required to drink it in the presence of the family and friends.

Pregnant women in Ethiopia are considered very fragile and are watched closely by family and friends. They seldom work beyond their first trimester, for fear work will exhaust Mamas-to-be and have a negative effect on the baby's health.

Ethiopian Mamas are also required to stay in bed for several weeks after the baby is born. Relatives and friends care for the baby while Mama recuperates. No need to rush back to work, they understand that Mama's body needs time to heal and she needs time to bond with her newborn.

chapter fourteen

hush little baby, please don't cry

Nothing pulls at a Mama's heartstrings more than the sound of a baby crying, especially her own. What's even more frustrating is when she can't figure out just what it is her baby wants.

As the baby grows older, Mama learns how to listen closely to the cry to determine just what's troubling her little one. Yet, this takes practice and patience. So, in the meantime, take these tips from me and other Mamas who swear they know what a baby wants and needs simply by the sound and pitch of the cry.

◆ A high-pitched yelp means the baby is hungry.

   Translation: "I'm hungry and cranky and if you don't give me my bottle right now, you will have no peace."

◆ A series of whimpering cries means the baby is tired or possibly uncomfortable.

   Translation: "Mama, you've kept me at the mall way too long and I am ready to go home and go to sleep."

◆ A moaning, monotonous cry means the baby is cranky.

Translation: "I am sick and tired of watching that goofy purple dinosaur and his happy friends, who never fight over toys or who will wear what costume."

◆ A long, continuous moan means the baby feels rejected.

Translation: "Okay, you've been watching Oprah and on the telephone gossiping way too long. It's time to give me a little attention."

◆ A whiny cry means the baby need a diaper change.

Translation: "My diaper is drenched and if you don't change me in the next five minutes, I will drop a dime to child services."

So the next time your baby cries, listen closely. No one knows a baby's needs better than his own Mama. It took me a while, but I finally figured out my son's whimpers and cries. And you know what? There were plenty of times when he wasn't wet, hungry, or neglected—I think he just cried for the hell of it.

Singing to Your Baby Will Soothe His Soul

ith a magical voice like Grammy Award–winning gospel singer CeCe Winans, you would think she could soothe any baby's soul! Whether CeCe is singing duets with her brother BeBe or her friend Whitney Houston, her voice is angelic, crisp, clear, and oooh-so-beautiful. She has fans across the country and CeCe has been known to bring tears of joy to the eyes of many who listen.

Besides her Grammy Awards, the songstress has racked up honors from the *Essence* and Stella Award committees. She has wowed thousands of adoring fans from Radio City Music Hall to the Omni in New Orleans. So you would think her baby boy, Alvin, would love her voice as much as her fans do.

Not! The first time CeCe tried to serenade Baby Alvin with a few verses of "Jesus Loves Me," he just didn't want any part of it. There was no smiling or cooing. Baby Alvin busted out crying. Alvin's famous Mama was heartbroken and completely baffled. Singing to soothe a baby's soul may work for some Mamas, but for CeCe, it seemed to be just an old wives' tale.

And if it didn't work for CeCe, I can't imagine it working for *anyone*—because we all know that girlfriend can sho' nuf *sang*. But suit yourself, it's certainly worth a try.

No More Tears

I don't care what anyone tells you, even the world's best Mamas will have those moments—which sometimes turn into hours—when their babies will not stop crying no matter what they do. Believe me, it *will* happen to you!

You've changed his diaper, given him a bottle, and tried to put him to sleep. You've sung to him, *yes, even the Barney song,* bounced him on your lap, and burped him, but nothing seems to soothe your infant's soul.

Well, don't fret—you definitely are not alone. Here are some tips from Mamas young and old on how to get your baby to stop crying:

- **Turn on the hair dryer or vacuum cleaner.** The sound will distract the baby.

- **Take the baby in the bathroom and run the shower.** Hearing the water and watching it flow just might put her to sleep.

- **Take baby for a ride.** Whether you put him in the car for a ride around the block or take him up and down on the elevator in your apartment building, the motion will help quiet him down.

- **Turn on some music.** It is sure to soothe her soul.

- **Click on the television.** The sudden introduction of un-familiar voices and pictures just might distract him enough to make him forget about the tears.

- **Swaddle the baby in a blanket.** When a baby is wrapped tight, it reminds him of being in his Mama's womb.

- **Take the baby outside for a walk.** The fresh air and new surroundings may be just what she needs.

- **Rub an ice cube on baby's hand.** The surprise of some-thing cold and wet on baby's skin just might make her happy again.

- **Clap your hands and hum a song.** It doesn't matter whether or not you can carry a tune, your baby will get a kick out of this.

- **Place a fish tank in baby's room.** The motion of the fish swimming in the water just might mesmerize your little bundle of joy.

chapter fifteen

what every new mama needs to know

Once you've mastered the basics of Mamahood—like changing diapers, feeding your baby, and keeping him or her on schedule—you'll still find yourself bombarded with questions every step of the way. Each day is a new learning experience, but to help you along, I've compiled this collection of fun, offbeat, and practical advice.

Insider's Information

- If you tickle the bottom of a baby's feet, it will cause the baby to stutter.

- If you obeyed your Mama, your child will obey you.

- If you let your baby look at you when you're over his head, the baby will become cross-eyed.

- Don't feed baby without testing the formula or food yourself.

- Always boil water before giving it to baby.

- If you cut your baby boy's hair before his first birthday, he will have a speech impediment and probably stutter.

- If you allow babies and small children to cross their eyes, they will get stuck like that.

Mummy Knows Best

ne of Mama's first concerns when she gets home is how she's gonna lose the weight. When Lizbeth was pregnant in the late forties, she was told by her Mama that if she wanted to keep her size-five figure, she would have to bind her body immediately after the baby was born.

"Bind my body?" Lizbeth asked.

"Yes, bind it," her Mama said. "You gotta tightly wrap white towels and sheets around your stomach, hips, and thighs and keep it secured with safety pins. The binding will get your skin nice and tight again and you will regain your shape before you know it."

Following her Mama's instructions, Lizbeth kept herself wrapped up like a mummy whenever she was alone or about to go to sleep. In a flash, Lizbeth was back into her favorite powder-blue-knit, size-five dress—just like her Mama promised.

Years later, when Lizbeth became a grandmother, she gave her daughters the same advice. "Bind your body," Lizbeth advised. "Believe me, it works."

Lizbeth's oldest daughter thought it was a little strange, but tried it anyway. She, too, wrapped up like a mummy faithfully every night before she went to sleep. And, like her Mama, she was as slim as she used to be in no time at all.

But her youngest daughter refused to wrap herself in sheets or towels.

"She laughed at me and told me I was nutty as a fruitcake," Lizbeth said. "She refused to try any old-time rituals."

Lizbeth urged her daughter to bind her body and rattled off dozens of success stories throughout the generations. None of the women in Lizbeth's family weighed more than 125 pounds; and all got their girlish figures back thanks to a ritualized pattern of body binding. Yet, even still, Lizbeth's daughter laughed at the thought of wrapping up like a mummy.

"Well, she should have listened to her Mama," Lizbeth said. "She's fat as a cow these days. Serves her right, 'cause Mama always knows best. I'm sixty-six years old and I still weigh one hundred ten pounds, just like I did in my youth."

If Your Child Is Alert and Bright, It's Making Room for the Next Child to Be Born

enya from Nashville was a dynamo baby—walking and talking before her first birthday. By the time her second birthday rolled around, Kenya was already reciting the alphabet.

When Kenya was three, she could read simple phrases and spoke perfect English. Kenya also dutifully cared for her dog, Jazz. Though many people assumed Kenya was a genius, her grandMama knew exactly what was going on.

"Kenya is beyond her years," her grandMama explained. "That means she is making room for your next child."

Kenya's parents were thrilled about the revelation. Three months later, Kenya's Mama found out that sure enough, she did indeed have a bun in the oven. As delighted as they were, they still were a bit hesitant. How would Kenya feel about a little baby brother or sister?

One night, Kenya's Mama and dad cut her a big slice of sweet potato pie and sat her down to tell her the good news.

"Sweetie, pretty soon you are going to have a little sister or brother," her Mama said. "You will have to help us take care of the baby, just like you help us with Jazz."

Kenya was so excited that she couldn't finish eating. She just rushed upstairs to start making room for the new baby.

"GrandMama was right," Kenya's Mama said. "Kenya couldn't be happier. What if this baby turns out to be as smart as Kenya? Will that mean *another* one is coming?"

"I guess we'll just have to wait and see," said the proud daddy, rubbing his wife's belly. "We'll see."

Wash Bowlegged Babies in Dishwater to Straighten Out Their Legs

here was a young Mama in Bridgeport, Alabama, in the early twenties who gave birth to a little bowlegged boy. The boy was so bowlegged that doctors feared he would not be able to walk, run, jump, and play with other kids when he got older.

The Mama took her son to see a specialist in Montgomery; he suggested surgery. Though reluctant at first, the boy's Mama didn't want her son to go through life walking with a waddle. After several visits to the specialist, she agreed to have the boy's legs operated on.

But, unfortunately, the first surgery was unsuccessful. Instead, the doctor put braces on his legs to attempt to straighten them out. Six months later, the braces came off, but, alas, his legs were still bowed.

The mother prayed for her son and asked for divine intervention. She waited and trusted that somehow a miracle would come.

Meanwhile, an elderly neighbor who baby-sat the little boy told the young mother to wash her son's legs in greasy dishwater every night.

"It will straighten out his legs in no time," she said.

The mother laughed out loud; figured she was crazy. The old lady explained that her mother was from Africa and this cure was widely believed in. The mother continued to laugh, and said thanks, but no thanks. Months passed and the boy's legs were still crooked and twisted. So each time the baby-sitter bathed the little boy, she would melt a little grease from her grease cup and pour it into his bathwater. As he splashed around the sink, the woman would massage his legs in the greasy, sudsy water.

A few months later, the mother started to notice her son's legs straightening out. She took him back to the doctors but they could not explain it. When she picked up the boy one day, she asked the sitter if she noticed a change.

"Of course I do," the sitter replied.

"I knew his legs would eventually straighten out," the mother said. "It was just a matter of time."

"No, it was a matter of fact," the sitter said.

"What do you mean?"

"Fact is that I've been bathing your boy in greasy dishwater for months," the sitter said. "You laughed at me when I told you 'bout it, but it worked. If the doctors can't figure it out, sometimes you must call on help from our ancestors."

The young mother was so thankful that she kissed the sitter and held her tight.

"I will never doubt the wisdom of my elders," the mother said. "Thank you so much. I will share this story with my son when he gets older."

If You Expose Your Unborn Baby to Intellectuals, Their Intelligence Will Rub Off on the Baby

Long before it was politically correct for pregnant mothers to read to their unborn children, actress Irma Hall's grandMama, whom she lovingly called "Mama," was convinced that by exposing herself to intellectual people, their intelligence would pass through the womb and rub off on her babies. Whenever she was pregnant—I'm talking all thirteen times—she attended forums, lectures, and every educational event she could find hoping her unborn baby would absorb tons of knowledge.

Mama even worked with black nationalist Marcus Garvey, a Jamaican-born man who came to the United States in 1916 to encourage black Americans to be proud of their African roots and strive for self-determination. Mama was convinced that by working with Garvey, the baby she was carrying at the time would not only be smart but would also be proud of his African-American heritage.

And guess what? Mama's intuition paid off. All of her children turned out to be smart as whips, and all thirteen kids graduated from college—a huge accomplishment for African-Americans in the late 1920s. They include a lawyer, a scientist, a nurse, and several entrepreneurs—all are grateful to "Mama" for giving them a head start in life.

Girls Who Give Their Mama Grief Get It Back

ack in the 1930s, Gussie Mae's Mama always warned her daughters that if they gave their Mama grief, they would later regret it. "It's widely known that girls who give their Mama grief will have twice as many problems with their own daughters someday."

Well, that didn't bother Gussie Mae one bit. She had always been a very obedient and loving girl and never gave her Mama a problem. But Gussie Mae's sister, Lema, was a terror as a child, so when she found out she was pregnant with twin girls at a young age, Mama's words came back to haunt her.

For it was Lema who took their Mama through difficult changes. She was a defiant child, who always did things her own way—no matter what the consequences. In grade school, Lema was a regular fixture in the disciplinarian's office—she talked back to teachers, cheated on tests, and once even got caught pulling the fire alarm.

As a teenager, Lema got worse. She sneaked out her bedroom window to go to the juke joints, danced all night, and slept during church every Sunday morning.

And when their Mama noticed that her moonshine had been slowly disappearing from the kitchen cabinet, Mama got a switch and tore up Lema's 'hine without asking any questions.

"You gon' be sorry," Gussie Mae always warned Lema. "Mama said our daughters will give us the same hell we gave her, even worse."

Lema didn't pay her sister any mind.

"That's just Mama's way of cutting back our fun," Lema often said. "She just wants us to go to church and be boring."

Boy, did Lema regret those words. Turns out Mama was right, as usual.

"Lema's twin girls came into the world raisin' hell and never stopped." Gussie Mae laughed. "Mama told us some crazy tales, but this one rings true. I never did ask Mama what kind of hell she caused grandMama, but she couldn't have been no angel or else the stork would have dropped Lema off at somebody else's house."

chapter sixteen

home remedies and cure-alls for babies and toddlers

Before there were antibiotics, ointments, and drops, Mama relied heavily on the land and her surroundings to cure her baby's ailments. Everything from tree bark to kerosene was used as a cure-all.

Even today, many Mamas are interested in returning to a more natural, wholesome lifestyle, especially when it comes to their newborns. And though I do believe some cure-alls and home remedies from the old days may work, others are just downright dangerous. Regressing to the old days is not the solution. Mamas have to use their common sense. However, the remedies are still fun to hear, so I'd like to share some with you that African-American women told me. These women reached back into their own childhood and early days of Mamahood to come up with this list of cure-alls.

Some of these *really* worked for me, but I must admit I was taken aback by many. Some made me laugh, others made me wince, but I am sure you will immediately recognize the ones that are just too old, too risky, or too offbeat to try. Please don't try any on your baby without first consulting your doctor or health professional.

Bones

A teaspoon of olive oil daily will insure that your baby has strong bones.

Bruises and Cuts

Long ago, before there were Band-Aids and antiseptic, when children had a cut, Mamas would wrap a spiderweb around the wound or mix a handful of soot from a chimney with lard and smear it on the cut to stop the bleeding.

Chicken Pox

If your infant or child has chicken pox, give him a bath in a tub of cold oatmeal to soothe the itching and give the child some relief.

Colds

As we all know, there's still no cure for the common cold. So what do you do when your baby is sniffling and sneezing and crying? Try these home remedies:

Give baby a half teaspoon of cod-liver oil daily. It was widely believed that the oil would grease the baby's insides and move the cold through the body faster.

Mix a handful of talcum with crushed onions and rub it on the baby's chest to get rid of a cold.

In the early 1900s, Mamas used to make cough drops from turpentine and kerosene. I don't have the recipe, but I would <u>not</u> give it to you if I did. This one should stay rooted in history.

Boil mutton, skim the fat off the water, and let it harden. Once the fat is thick, rub it on the baby's chest.

A group of Caribbean Mamas had their own remedies to combat the common cold. Here's what they suggested:

> Crush garlic and sprinkle it into a pot of boiling water. Add sugar and let it cool off.
> Mix eucalyptus oil with a half teaspoon of white rum and a cup of warm water.
> Mix honey with the juice of a raw onion and give it to the baby.

Coughing

> Mix a quarter cup of honey, a quarter cup of vinegar, and a cup of warm water and give to baby.
> Dissolve a large piece of rock candy into a cup of tea and have baby drink it warm.
> Heat two teaspoons of dark whiskey with a half teaspoon of sugar and a cup of water. Give the baby a few sips.
> Mix a tablespoon of ground ginger with a pinch of sugar and a few drops of lemon juice. Add water to dilute and give to baby to drink.
> Add a tablespoon of whiskey to a hot cup of tea.

Once your child's cold is cured, you just might need a little *something-something* to jump-start him and get your baby peppy again. Here's what Willie Mae used to do back in the days when . . .

Willie Mae had three children back in the 1930s. Each time one of her babies or toddlers suffered from a bad cold or infection, she would give them a half teaspoon of corn liquor or white whiskey to give them a little pep. It was a family tradition that Willie Mae's great-grandmother picked up from her neighbor in Roanoke, Virginia, back in the early 1900s. She passed it down to her daughters and the tradition is still going strong today.

Just last year, when Willie Mae's granddaughter was recovering from a cold, she told her daughter to give the child a tiny swig of liquor.

"A little moonshine increases the baby's stamina and rejuvenates the child," Willie Mae said. "The child will be moving around like she was never sick in no time."

Sure enough, the little girl was her bouncy, smiling self in no time—thanks to (or in spite of) Grandma Willie Mae's sound advice.

Colic

Before there were Mylicon Drops, Mama had her own way of dealing with a colicky baby. And each remedy is as different as the women who shared them.

> Give baby a bottle filled with warm water and a few drops of brandy.
> Rub baby's stomach, then hold baby upside down to allow gas to pass through the body.
> Sprinkle asafetida (a gum resin from the roots of certain plants that has a horrible odor) into a piece of sheet and tie a knot. Attach a string to the asafetida bag and tie it around the baby's neck. Every hour, rotate the bag on and off the baby's neck. (This may have been very popular in the twenties and thirties, but don't tie anything around a baby's neck.)
> Place a hot water bag filled with warm water on baby's stomach.

Hold the baby above your head and gently rock him back and forth. The movement will calm baby and make him stop crying.

Place baby across your knee and rub her back in a circular motion with the palm of your hand.

Boil the leaves of a tomato plant, let it cool, and give it to your baby to drink.

Give the baby an eight-ounce bottle filled with warm water and a teaspoon of molasses.

Give the baby a warm bottle of milk mixed with a half teaspoon of whiskey and a dash of asafetida.

Massage the baby's stomach with warm castor oil.

Add one drop of kerosene and one drop of asafetida to warm water, Carnation milk, or breast milk. (Do NOT try this one, either! It should stay rooted in history.)

Now, don't fret if none of these home remedies work for you. Jordan was colicky and I finally came up with a solution. . . .

Another name for colic is the gripes. Black women from around the globe say only a bottle of gripe water—a sweet-tasting syrup imported from England or Jamaica that has a small amount of alcohol—will cure the gripes.

My son, Jordan, suffered terribly from colic. I had tried the over-the-counter Mylicon Drops, but to no avail. Jordan was in pain and screaming at the top of his lungs for hours at a time. His nanny, Dolly, and I were tired of walking him around the apartment, rubbing his stomach, and placing a hot water bag on his stomach.

Finally, I called Jordan's doctor. He said only that babies will eventually outgrow colic, and suggested over-the-counter drops. By that time, I was desperate.

"In my country [Guyana], we give babies gripe water to relieve the gripes," Dolly said. "They don't recommend it in this country, because it has alcohol in it."

"Will it harm Jordan in any way?" I asked.

"No, there's no need to worry," Dolly reassured me. "They sell gripe water in Korean grocery stores."

We had one little problem. Finding a Korean grocery store in the middle of the suburbs was impossible. In fact, we had to drive several miles into Manhattan in order to purchase a bottle of the white syrup.

Right after Dolly gave Jordan the gripe water, he stopped crying and passed a lot of gas. Now, I swear by gripe water. It was the only relief for Jordan's colic.

Complexion

Wipe the baby's face with a urine-soaked diaper to clear up blotches and insure a smooth complexion. Sounds gross and unhygienic, I know, but it worked for Jordan.

Bathe baby in a tub filled with warm water and a tiny bit of borax to keep baby's skin beautiful and soft.

Wash baby's face with Pear soap daily to keep his complexion smooth.

Congestion

Squeeze a few tiny drops of saline solution in baby's nose.

Roll up a thick towel or baby blanket and place it under the mattress of the baby's crib—where the baby lays his head.

Constipation

To relieve your baby of constipation, add a teaspoon of dark Karo syrup to his formula.

Take a bar of Ivory soap, cut a sliver off the end and make sure it comes to a soft point. Wet the tip of the soap sliver and rub it around the baby's anus. Within minutes, the baby will have a bowel movement.

Give the baby a bottle of the juice of collard greens diluted with a little water.

Give the baby a warm bottle of water with two tablespoons of prune juice.

Give the baby a warm bottle of water with a half teaspoon of molasses.

Give the baby a warm bottle of bluegrass herbal tea.

Cradle Cap

If your baby suffers from cradle cap, rub mineral oil into his scalp and massage it.

Carefully pick the flakes from baby's head with an infant comb.

Wash hair, dry it thoroughly, and apply a light hair grease to scalp.

Crib Death or Sudden Infant Death Syndrome

Lie baby on its side with a rolled-up towel in front of baby and behind baby to keep him or her from rolling on stomach.

Check on baby regularly while he or she is napping.

This is a very scary disease, and though there is no known cure, most mothers have some fear of crib death.

Four beautiful young sisters from Ethiopia who I met on an airplane told me that new Mamas in Ethiopia are just as concerned about crib death. When their youngest sister was born, the girls were teenagers. "Our mother was so afraid of crib death that one of us was forced to stay in the room with our baby sister at all times," one sister told me.

"Yeah, we sat there around the clock," another chimed in. "We couldn't read a book or anything, we had to literally stare at the baby to make sure she was still breathing."

According to them, it wasn't an easy assignment. In fact, it was so boring, they often caught each other sleeping on the job. They said they told their Mama how ridiculous it was, but the more they complained, the longer their shift got.

"We used to be so mad," one sister said. "Imagine sitting in a room staring at a baby all day when you would rather be outside with your friends or doing anything else."

Their baby sister is now a healthy teenager and they love her dearly, but they think their Mama was a bit over the top—requesting them to keep watch around the clock. My advice is to keep a close eye on baby and say a prayer.

Croup

If your baby has croup, crush an onion and fill the baby's bottle with the juice. Add a little water to dilute it. After the baby drinks the onion juice, steam up the bathroom and sit in there for ten minutes.

Rub the baby down with Vicks and take him into a steamy bathroom. Sit in there for at least thirty minutes.

Diaper Rash

Sprinkle a little cornstarch or flour on the baby before diapering him.

Sprinkle a little baby powder before diapering him.

Rub Vaseline or A&D Ointment on baby's genitals.

Add a dash of baking soda to the baby's bathwater.

Diarrhea

Give the baby (obviously not a newborn) small pieces of burnt toast.

Take a fresh coconut, slice it, fry it, and add a teaspoon of salt. Drain the oil and let it cool off. Use a dropper to give the coconut oil to baby.

Ear Infection

Release a few drops of the baby's urine in its ear to get rid of ear infections. Some Mamas still claim this works, but I would suggest checking with the baby's doctor first.

Fever

Every hour for fifteen minutes, place a white potato under the baby's arm to get rid of fever.

Dice an onion and put chunks in baby's socks or shoes to get rid of fever.

Rub the baby down with ice cubes and/or place the child into a tub of cool water.

Rub the baby down with rubbing alcohol.

Headache

When your baby is born, cut a piece of his hair and bury it under a rock so he will never have a headache.

Hiccups

Down in Tallahassee, Mamas swear that if you place a wet piece of brown paper bag on the baby's forehead, the hiccups will go away.

In Charlotte, Mamas say the piece of bag doesn't have to be wet, just a plain brown paper bag will do.

Place a spoonful of sugar under the baby's tongue and his hiccups will go away.

Place a piece of straw from a broom over the baby's head, and it will cure the hiccups. This was passed down from West African mothers to slaves.

An eight-year-old girl named Brandi suggests that you sneak up behind the baby to scare the hiccups away.

My Mama said to let the baby suck on his bottle and that's the end of story. This one worked for me!

Hives

A few sips of herbal tea may help cure the hives.

Rub calamine lotion on baby.

Jaundice

Long ago, if your baby was born with jaundice, you were told to ask a farmer to scrape the horn of a cow and drop the scrapings into a quart of boiling water. After it cooled, you were told to put the liquid in a bottle and give it to your baby to cure jaundice. Today, I'd see a doctor.

Expose baby to sunlight by sitting outdoors with him on the porch, park bench, or balcony.

Navel

Grease baby's navel cord with castor oil and it will fall off.
Tape a silver dollar to the baby's belly button to make it go in.
Wrap a bellyband around the baby's stomach to help the
belly button contract.

Nose Bleed

Take a piece of brown paper bag and place it on the baby's
tongue to stop the bleeding.

Teething

Rub a drop of brandy or whiskey on the baby's gums.
Rub an ice cube on the baby's gums.
Let the baby gnaw on a chicken bone or rib bone.
Give the baby a rubber teething ring.
In the old days, if your baby needed relief from teething,
you'd be advised to tie a string of hog's teeth around its
neck. Obviously, today, we know not to tie anything
around a baby's neck for fear of choking.
Dominican Mamas said they use a tonic called Cordial de
Monel to relax the baby and ease the pain.

Thrush

Wet a piece of cloth with lime water and wipe the inside of
baby's mouth.
Wipe the inside of baby's mouth with glycerin.

Whooping Cough

Generations ago, Mamas believed that if you let a cat drink
out of a bowl of milk, then put the rest in the baby's bottle, the whooping cough would be cured. I doubt it.

chapter seventeen

mama and me

As you've figured out by now, babies need constant care and attention . . . and there are times when you'll need to be in five places at once. Here are some easy tips on traveling, transporting, and bringing up your baby to love and adore you.

Have Baby, Will Travel

Two months after giving birth to a bouncing little baby boy, an executive named Alvis returned to her job, which required her to travel all over the country.

When she was sent to the Bahamas for a conference, Alvis took her son and husband along. After a pleasant flight, Alvis and her family checked into their hotel. The oceanfront room had all the comforts of home, but there was one problem—there was no baby's crib. Alvis called her Mama back home and she quickly solved the problem.

"Just open the bottom dresser drawer, pad it with a pillow and a blanket, and tuck little Jacob in," her Mama said. "I know he will sleep just fine."

Alvis was a little reluctant at first, but Mama was right, Baby Jacob slept peacefully through the night.

"It's much more convenient than traveling with a bassinet," Alvis confessed. "Now, all my friends are doing the same thing. It's just one less thing to worry about when you travel with an infant."

Baby in a Basket

n the old days, Mamas used to venture into woodsy areas of Africa to gather twigs, branches, and mud in order to hand-weave baskets. The baskets were mainly used to transport fruits and vegetables, but they were also used for babies.

African babies not only slept in the beautiful baskets but they also were often carried around in them. Once the baby outgrew the basket, the Mama would continue to use the basket for her daily duties.

When my friend Kelly heard about that, she decided that her newborn would sleep in a straw basket. Instead of spending money to buy a bassinet, she lined a basket with foam and placed several receiving blankets on top of it. Then, Kelly placed her little bundle of joy into the basket.

Kelly was so pleased with the idea that she began decorating baskets for her pregnant friends. Kelly decorated one friend's basket with authentic kente cloth, and another friend's, who was expecting a girl, with pink satin and chiffon.

She then filled each straw basket with baby goodies—like bibs, bottles, and diapers—and gave them for shower gifts. Kelly's gift was a hit and she owed it all to the proud African women who wove their baskets and toted their babies from place to place. And after Kelly's daughter outgrew the beautiful basket, her Mama filled the basket with her stuffed animals and books and displayed it proudly in her room next to the baby's crib.

Location, Location, Location

veryone knows the golden rule of real estate—"Location, location, location"—but did you know that the location of your home may also have a profound effect on your baby's personality, appearance, and disposition?

Whether you live in the hills, near a body of water, or smack-dab in the middle of the city, your newborn will be affected by his surroundings. Here's what black women from all across the country have told me. . . .

- ◆ If you live in the desert, your baby's complexion will be dark, smooth, and beautiful.

- ◆ If you live in the city, your baby will be bubbly, energetic, and a tad bit boisterous.

- ◆ If you live high in the mountains, your baby will be warm-blooded, adventurous, and free-spirited.

- ◆ If you live near a body of water, your baby will be content, peaceful, and welcoming to others.

- ◆ If you live in a woodsy area, your baby will be timid, meek, and shy.

- ◆ If you live in the suburbs, your baby will be soft-spoken, inquisitive, and laid back.

The Joy of Mamahood

et's face it, Mamahood is a beautiful experience, but it's not always easy. Just keep in mind, if you think it's hard to be a mother today, remember our ancestors. Mamahood during slavery was extremely difficult. Slave women were forced to work in the fields up until the very minute they delivered. Within hours of birth, some mothers were sent back out to work, while the newborns were placed either under a tree near their mother, or in the care of elderly women who nursed dozens of other slave babies at a time.

Mamas and fathers prayed daily that slavery would be abolished and their kids would lead better lives. But until then, they came up with new and creative ways to try to ease their children's hardships. Though most slaves worked in the fields, some were chosen to work in the homes of wealthy white plantation owners—otherwise known as the "Big House"—helping to run the household.

The house jobs were hard to come by, and the majority were filled by slaves who were either light-skinned or who were the very best at their trade. So desperate were slaves to have their children work in the Big House that they went to extreme measures to help them get there. Slaves believed that their kids would have a better chance of landing a job in the Big House if they looked European, with straight noses and fine hair. Some slave Mamas would often rub oil on their infant's hair to keep it fine and straight—"good hair." They believed oils would prevent their child's hair from becoming kinky and nappy. And, sometimes, they would even take a clothespin and snap it on their child's nose to try to make it small and narrow.

Another habit slave mothers developed was checking the baby's ears and nail beds to see if the child's pigmentation would darken with age. If it was very light, it was believed the child would be light-skinned.

It's sad to say, but many of these nuances are still around today. When Jordan was born, several people reassured me that he would not get very dark—as if it was a big deal to me—they had checked his ears and nail beds.

A so-called friend of the family suggested that I pinch Jordan's nose because his nostrils were quite wide.

"I don't think so," I replied, politely. "Jordan is my African-American prince. His wide nose and kinky hair are part of our rich heritage."

In a conversation with an old Creole woman from New Orleans, she told me about a fair-skinned black woman who ran a day-care service out of her home on the bayou in the 1930s. This woman claimed she loved babies, but she was very selective in picking who would or wouldn't get in. As the story was told, she'd give each child the paper bag and comb tests to decide if she'd baby-sit them. If the baby's skin was lighter than a paper bag and she could get a fine-toothed comb through its hair, then that baby was accepted.

As far as African-Americans have come today, it's amazing that so many traditions from slavery are still lingering around. But what was most troubling is that some African-Americans still don't believe that black is indeed beautiful.

As we continue to define our roles in society, African-

American women—many of us are grandMas, Mamas, and daughters—are faced with the challenge of trying to raise children in a world that is still not free of racism, sexism, bigotry, and prejudice. The most important gift we can give our offspring is the love, confidence, and determination it will take to strive for greatness.

The spirit, strength, and beauty of our African heritage are awesome and we should celebrate them whenever possible. We must constantly remind our children of the positive characteristics they possess and magnificent contributions our ancestors have made to world culture.

Mama and Me

They say the apple doesn't fall far from the tree,
that sums it up for my Mama and me.

Ever since I was a little girl,
I admired Mama more than anyone in the world.

She taught me how to cook, mend, and clean,
Mama keeps the family together, she's our African queen.

A wonderful mother and also a great friend,
by my side until the bitter end.

We giggle together and always share,
wisdom, beauty, and love reflect Mama's care.

When I ask Mama for some motherly advice,
on how to be stern, but also protective, and nice.

She warns me not to spoil him or else he'll be a brat,
a whiny Mama's boy is not where it's at.

"You're a good Mama to your baby boy,
keep giving love and support to your bundle of joy."

Mama says Jordan reminds her of me when I was a girl,
the happiest little babies in all of the world.

Thank you, Mama, for being a great example for me,
you're the apple of my eye, the finest branch in our
family tree.